Manipulation and

*A complete guide to the art of persuasion,
overcoming panic attacks, and shielding yourself
from negativity using neuro-linguistic
programming*

JOHN B. MITCHEL

Table of Contents

Introduction

Every aspect of human life has two sides- positive and negative, but it depends on the human that how he or she utilizes it for their own good as well as for others. Consider manipulation as a part of dark psychology, and it is used greatly for the wrongdoings and harmful deeds. On the other side, it can be utilized in a positive way as well, but it's all in your own hand that how you want to utilize it. As far as persuasion is concerned, people use it in every field and part of life. For example, a salesman will always try to persuade you to buy his or her recommended product even if you do not want to. Persuasion also has two aspects of being applied. If you try to persuade a person to do something illegal or unethical that it is the part of dark psychology but if you persuade someone to get out or leave a certain thing that is not beneficial in any means, let's say suicide then you are using it for the good purpose. Everything you do or perceive is totally in the human mind, and you yourself are the controller of it. If you don't want to, then no one can make you do things without your will and consent. Also, it is an essential part of living life to observe your surroundings and the people who are around you.

If you do not notice the small things and interpret them wisely, then you are more likely to fall prey for something negative and hazardous. By observation such as facial expressions, body language, gestures, and the words and tone used can predict a lot about people if observed closely. If you fail to recognize such signals that are inclined towards the negativity, then you will be unable to keep yourself safe from them. Dark psychology is considered to be starting from the point where you have no intent or motive to do things, but for your own self-satisfaction and pleasure, and in return, it is damaging to the other person or even community. Every living individual has this dark side, but not all of them let that side overcome them. Once you are exposed to that side, there is no coming back. So always watch yourself and your surroundings so that you can keep yourself off of any harm.

Chapter 01: Manipulation

This technique knowingly or unknowingly is used by every human being to attain whatever he or she wants. It's the most common and daily routine example of is a child crying if he is not given what he wants. Every other person, whether a businessman, employee, peon, maids, they all manipulate one another for their personal benefits. Your partner will use a cute puppy face to manipulate you to do whatever he wants to even if that is for making another plan while he was already committed to you for dine out or anything like that. Emotional manipulation is vastly used by your closed ones or family members, even for the smallest of the chores. However, if this sort of manipulation is used, which is not harming anyone in any way possible, then it is acceptable.

But if you do something wrong or negative by manipulating, which includes blackmailing, that is totally not acceptable, and this inclines towards the dark psychology. I have mentioned all the checkmarks in detail to see for yourself if you are being manipulated for the wrong cause or the right one.

What Manipulation is?

Most individuals indulge in regular manipulation. For instance, telling someone you feel "fine" when you are sad or depressed is technically a type of manipulation as it controls the perceptions and reactions of your acquaintance towards you.

However, manipulation could also have more pernicious consequences and is often linked to emotional abuse, especially in loving relationships. Many other people perceive manipulation negatively, particularly when it damages the manipulated person's physical, emotional, or mental health.

While people that frequently manipulate others are doing so because individuals feel the desire to regulate their surroundings and environment, an urge often stemming from deep-seated anxiety and fear; this is not acceptable behavior.

Engaging in deception will keep the trickster from communicating with their own selves, and being deceived may contribute to a wide variety of ill effects being encountered.

1.1 Mental Health Manipulation Effects

Manipulation, if unaddressed, can give rise to mental health problems for those manipulated. Prolonged manipulation in good relationships could also be a sign of emotional abuse that can, in some cases, have a similar impact to trauma — especially when the perpetrator is forced to think guilty and ashamed.

Perpetrators of prolonged manipulation might:

• Try to please the above manipulative individual constantly

• Develop improper coping patterns

• Put the interests of another individual before yourself

• Feel depressed

• Lie about feelings

• Develop anxiety

• having trouble trusting people

Manipulation may, in some cases, be so omnipresent that it creates a victim to doubt their view of reality.

One such tale highlighted in the classic film Gaslight, in which a woman's husband slyly manipulated her till she no longer believed her own perspectives. For instance, the husband clandestinely turned the gaslights down & persuaded his wife that the flickering light was really in her head.

Manipulation In Light Of Mental Health

Although most individuals sometimes participate in coercion, persistent history of abuse may suggest an ongoing problem for mental well-being.

Manipulation is especially frequent with diagnoses of a personality disorder like (NPD) narcissistic personality as well as BPD borderline personality. Manipulation may be a way for those with BPD to satisfy their inner desires or get approval, which sometimes occurs when the individual with BPD perceives being abandoned or insecure. Although most individuals with BPD have experienced or witnessed abuse, manipulation might just have established indirectly as a mechanism for dealing with the needs. Individuals with an NPD may have various reasons for manipulative conduct.

Since those with NPD may struggle to form close relationships, individuals might even succumb to manipulation to "keep" their companion in the relationship.

Features of manipulative abuse can involve bullying, accusing, playing the "victim," problems of dominance, and gaslighting.

Proxy Munchausen syndrome, through which a caregiver induces another adult to become sick for affection or attention, is another disorder marked by manipulative behavior.

1.2 Manipulation in Relations

Prolonged manipulation, such as those among friends, family members, as well as intimate partners, can have severe effects in relationships. Manipulation can worsen a relationship's health & contribute to the mental health problems of those in the marriage or even relationship disintegration.

Manipulation could even cause one partner in matrimony or partnership to feel isolated, worthless, or bullied. Also, in stable partnerships, one spouse can exploit the other unintentionally to prevent conflict or even to try and protect their spouse from becoming burdened. Several individuals may even know that their relationship is being manipulated, but choose to disregard it or downplay it. Manipulation in interpersonal partnerships may take several types, including guilt, gift-giving, exaggeration, or the selective expression of love, passive aggression, and secrecy.

Parents who abuse their kids can set up their kids for depression, anxiety, guilt, eating disorders as well as some mental health problems. One research has shown that mother and father who use manipulation techniques on parenting children on a daily basis may actually raise the risk that their kids may use manipulative actions. Signs of manipulation in the relationship between parent and child may entail making the kid feel culpable, a parent's lack of responsibility, dismissing the progress of a child, and a requirement to be engaged in many areas of the kid's life.

People might also perceive manipulated when they're part of a toxic relationship. One individual can use the other in deceptive relationships to satisfy their own desires at the cost of their mate's. A dishonest friend may use remorse or manipulation to gain things such as borrowing funds, or they can approach the friend only when they want to fulfill their other emotional needs, and may seek reasons when the friend needs support.

1.3 Instances of Behavior Manipulation

Often, individuals can unintentionally control others without completely becoming informed of what they are doing, whilst others can deliberately seek to improve their coercion techniques.

Some signs of tampering include:

- Information is withheld

- Verbal abuse

- A human alienated from friends and family

- Passive Aggressive Actions

- Gaslighting

- Disparity

- Risks implicated

- Sex usage to attain goals

Seeing that the reasons behind deception may range from unintentional to deliberate, it is necessary to recognize the deceptive situations that are taking place. While breaking stuff off might also be crucial in abuse situations, a counselor may benefit others to learn how to deal with or address other people's behaviors.

1.4 How to Cope Manipulative Influence

When manipulation might become toxic, it can be exhausting to deal with other people's behavior. Workplace coercion has been found to affect efficiency, even loved one's manipulative actions may render truth seem doubtful. If you feel exploited in some kind of partnership, it may be beneficial to:

• **Rest assured.** Manipulation can sometimes include attempts by one person to cause another to question their skills, instinct, or even fact. If this occurs, keeping to the narrative will help; but, if this keeps happening in a strong relationship, it may be time to quit.

• **Hold on the subject.** When you call out a situation that leaves you feeling exploited, the other party can try to mitigate the problem or muddle the problem by manipulating other problems. Know to adhere to the point of view.

• **Disengage.** If somebody wants to get you a specific emotional reaction, decided not to hand it to them. For instance, if you are inclined to flatter a dishonest friend before requesting for an overbearing favor, don't play along —

rather, answer respectfully and continue the discussion forward.

- **Handle the situation.** The point on the manipulative conduct as it happens. Maintaining an emphasis on how the behavior of the other party impact you rather than beginning with an argumentative claim will often help you find a settlement whilst maintaining that the manipulation methods won't function with you.

1.5 Directing towards Manipulation in Counselling

Treatment and counseling for manipulative conduct that relies on the conduct trigger underlying problems. For example, whether the abuse is triggered by an internal mental health condition, interpersonal treatment may help the person realize that their behavior is harmful to themselves and others around them. A therapist will also be able to assist the manipulative individual in developing strategies to communicate with others while maintaining their limits and resolving underlying prejudices, which may lead to the behavior.

Some mental health problems, like borderline personality, can cause people to feel insecure about relationships, leading them to behave manipulatively to feel secure. In these situations, a therapist can help the individual resolve the mental health problem, which may, in effect, reduce their distress and make them feel comfortable in the relationships.

Chapter 02: The Manipulation Ethics

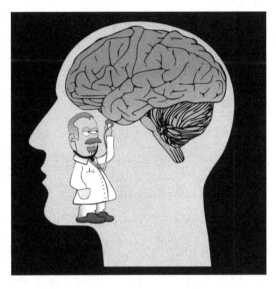

Everything comes with its own terms and conditions to be used and applied in daily life, whether it's any sort of electrical appliance or any other thing which is used physically. The same is the case with your words, emotions, dialogues, expressions, and all such things. Although these things do not come with the handbook to utilize or express them properly, the human brain is of great capabilities and can work in whichever way you want it to work. So to use manipulation in your own best possible way, I have discussed in this chapter that how you can conduct the manipulation and when it will be of the negative side. So keep a check on yourself and your everyday conduct with others.

2.1 Ethical Conduction of Manipulation

One can reasonably call every one of these strategies a type of manipulation. Many have much more precise, common names like "guilt trip," "gas-lighting," "peer pressure," "nagging," and "emotional blackmail." Maybe not everyone would agree that these tactics are accurately known as manipulation. And in some situations, whether the technique appears deceptive can depend on specific details not defined as stated in the case. For instance, if Y is deeply unethical, then it might not be deceptive for Irving to provoke Tonya to feel bad about planning to do Y. It's also probable that we could revisit our conclusions on any of these strategies in the light of a thoroughly worked-out and well-supported manipulation theory − if we got one. Nonetheless, in the current context, this description should give a fairly decent understanding of what we signify by "manipulation." This would also help to highlight the wide variety of widely defined techniques as exploitation.

Manipulation is frequently seen as a type of influence, which is neither exploitation nor reasonable persuasion.

But this interpretation immediately poses the question: Is any method of power that is not a form of intimidation, either coercion or logical persuasion? If manipulation doesn't really inhabit the whole logical space of impacts, which are neither reasonable persuasion nor extortion, then what does it distinguish from other aspects of influence, which are neither exploitation nor reasonable persuasion.

The term "manipulation" is typically believed to provide a component of moral disapproval: saying that Irving tricked Tonya is usually viewed as a moral critique of the behavior of Irving. Is there always immorality in manipulation? Why is it immoral? (When it is immoral) for? If coercion is not always unethical, then when it is unethical, what determines?

2.2 Preliminaries

Global vs. Ordinary Manipulation

In ordinary life, aspects of impact like those mentioned above are prevalent. This differentiates them from types of influence, which are described in the literature of free will as "manipulation." There, generally, the word "manipulation" applies to extreme conditioning or reprogramming of one or much of the values, preferences, and other mental conditions of an individual.

Such worldwide manipulation (as we would consider it) is also typically conceived as occurring through decidedly extraordinary methods, like supernatural intervention, specific neurological engineering, or radical indoctrination and mental conditioning programs. Usually, global exploitation is assumed to be depriving the target of independent will. This prevalent gut instinct drives the "manipulation argument" that seeks to protect incompatibility by claiming to have been the perpetrator of worldwide manipulation by living in a simulated reality.

Given the disparity among usual manipulation as well as the types of manipulation, the link between them is still worth questioning about. If global manipulation deprives the target of independent will or sovereignty entirely, could more specific types of coercion do anything similar, albeit on a more restricted scale? If Tonya falls prey to one of Irving's tactics, should we consider her less free — and perhaps less accountable — to do X?

2.3 Applications of an Ordinary Manipulation Theory

Manipulation has rarely been the topic of philosophical investigation in its own right until recently.

That being said, the truth that manipulation has been generally believed to weaken consent validity has spurred to its repeated acknowledgment in aspects where validity consent is at stake.

One such unit is healthcare ethics, where the conditions proposed for independent explicit consent almost always refer to the demand to make sure permission isn't really manipulated. In reality, one of the best known consistent philosophical discussions on manipulation appears in the influential book, by Nancy King, Ruth Faden, and Tom Beauchamp. Medical ethicists widely hold the perspective that manipulation nullifies the legitimacy of consent. There is, however, far less consensus about how to evaluate if a given type of impact is manipulative. That inadequacy of agreement is nowhere more evident than in the latest "nudges" discussions.

Cass Sunstein & Richard Thaler introduced the notion of a nudge to relate to the intentional launch of non-coercive, subtle, impacts into people's decision making in order to get them to make more optimum choices. Some nudges solely focus on providing better and more understandable data; these nudges appear best defined as influences which enhance the quality of reasonable deliberation.

But some nudges perform through psychological mechanisms, whose relation to reasonable deliberation is at best questionable. Most of these nudges manipulate biases in reasoning, decision-making, and heuristics, as well as numerous different psychological procedures operating outside consciousness. For instance, some evidence indicates that individuals are quite likely to select a procedure if they have been told it has a sustenance rate of 90 % rather than a mortality rate of 10 percent. Is it really deceptive for a doctor to manipulate this twisting impact to push the person in making the best-considered decision? Is it deceptive to put healthier food products at eye level for a lunchroom supervisor to get customers to choose them? The query of whether & when the manipulation of nudges has triggered a heated discussion.

Some nudge advocates suggest that there is hardly anything manipulative regarding portraying such decision making in one manner instead of another as it is often extremely difficult to define a decision without trying to point the decision-maker in some way. For starters, physicians must have details regarding the result either in terms of the risk of fatality or the probability of life (and, whether they provide both, they must provide one first), & cafeteria operators must pick what to place in the displays at eye level. This being so, why do you think it is dishonest to intentionally pick one form to portray the choice over the other? Some nudge defenders suggest that doing it on purpose is not manipulative in instances where it is unavoidable to incorporate an illogical impact into decision-making. Even though there are explanations to be skeptical of this mode of thinking, suppose Jones is going to travel on the subway car to a work interview so packed with people that it's inevitable he'll stumble up towards other travelers. Suppose he capitalizes on this fact to intentionally stumble out the door of his competing job applicant as it closes, making sure he'll be late for his interview. Evidently, the reality that some stumbling was inevitable on Jones' part doesn't really excuse Jones' deliberate bumping with his competitor. Likewise, even if we undoubtedly implement non-rational impacts into the decision-making of one another, that truth seems inadequate to verify that such impacts just cannot be manipulative. This idea is undoubtedly flawed, but it should be enough to start questioning the supposition that an intentional nudge isn't really manipulative just because another nudging is sure to happen.

More complex debates on how nudges are manipulative seem to rely less on the unavoidable consequence of nudging in one area or another, & also on the processes through which nudging happens, as well as the direction through which it drives the nudging individual towards. While there is broad consensus that certain nudges could be manipulative, there has been no consensus regarding which nudges have become manipulative or even how to distinguish among manipulative from non-manipulative nudges.

Questions over nudges' legitimacy go far beyond the healthcare setting. But apart from the healthcare industry, Sunstein and Thaler advocate of its utilization by government, employers & other entities. The government's use of nudges raises further concerns, particularly regarding the paternalistic approach behind them. The political theorists, as well as philosophers, have often posed concerns regarding certain ways of coercion in the democratic realm. Ancient Greek figures like Thrasymachus and Callicles can be traced back to the idea that political persons might achieve, keep political authorities by means such that we might now say are manipulative. Not only does Niccolo Machiavelli give details, but he advises political strategies that we might probably consider manipulative.

The far more philosophical focus in the domain of business ethics has been based on the issue of whether marketing is manipulative. The analyst John Galbraith reportedly called advertising "the manipulation of customer inclination" and contrasted being the focus of marketing with being assaulted by demons that ingrained in him an enthusiasm often for silk clothing, sometimes even for kitchenware, and often for chamber pots sometimes even for orange squash.

Several thinkers made similar advertising critiques. These critiques are often confined to types of advertising which do not merely demonstrate precise factual data. It seems challenging to claim, as is the story with solely informational nudges, that advertising which does nothing other than signifying that accurate factual data is manipulative.

However, most advertisement seeks to manipulate customer behavior through certain methods than or even in addition to offering strictly specific facts. These non-informative ads are the most suitable vehicle for exploitation issues. Roger Crisp and Tom Beauchamp made impactful assertions that advertising such as this could be manipulative. Similar critiques argue that non-informative ads will subvert sovereignty or improperly disrupt the wishes of customers, e.g., Santilli. Such criticisms either are variants of or relatives or advertising critique as manipulation. On the other hand, Robert Arrington asserts that advertising, in fact, very rarely manipulates its viewers, or undermines the autonomy of its audience. A massive amount of empirical evidence has been marshaled by Michael Phillips to claim that although some marketing strategy is manipulative, its own critiques greatly overstate its ability to influence buyers.

2.4 Two Manipulation Questions

As would be obvious from our conversation thus far, two key concerns regarding deception have to be addressed. Both should answer a satisfying concept of manipulation. One problem – name it the issue of identity – involves description and recognition: How do we classify the types of power that are deceptive and those who aren't? A reasonable answer will necessarily require a general manipulation concept, which illustrates what the different types of manipulative control have in common. An answer to the definition problem would also include guidelines for evaluating if a particular instance of the control is deceptive, in addition to highlighting whether the different instances of coercion are examples of a common, more fundamental phenomenon. Such a review could, of course, reveal that a few of the anomalies which we were already reluctant to consider as deception are crucially distinct from obvious instances of manipulation, such that we could be guided to rethink our use of the word "manipulation," at least in situations where specificity is essential.

The second problem— label it the problem of assessment — affects morality: how can we determine manipulation's moral status? A reasonable answer to one such query should inform us whether there is always immorality in manipulation. And if coercion isn't necessarily unethical, a correct approach to the problem of judgment will teach us how to decide whether it's unethical. More specifically, though, a reasonable explanation of judgment would clarify whether coercion becomes unethical when it becomes immoral. What feature in deception renders it unethical because it is illegal in such situations?

While the issues relevant to recognition and assessment are separate, these are not completely different. Any study of whether deception is unethical (when unethical) must require any understanding of what deception is. So our explanation of identification will restrict our conclusion of the evaluation. But an explanation of identification could do more than restrict our explanation of evaluation: it could guide it too. If a manipulation account defines the fundamental trait for being relevantly identical to something else that we have different justification for finding to be fundamentally incorrect, then we would generally claim that manipulation seems to be completely wrong for precisely that reason. Ultimately, we may have to change our responses to just one of these queries if they mean implausible together. Of starters, if we describe manipulation as any form of influence in addition to reasonable persuasion or intimidation, and then say that the absurdity of manipulation is total, we will be compelled to infer that almost no type of influence but rational persuasion is morally ever valid. This is a controversial hypothesis that some would be ready to accept, but it is a premise that comes by integrating some response to the problem of identity with some response to the question of assessment.

2.5 Answering the question of identification

There are currently three main features of manipulation: One deals with manipulation as that of an impact which diminishes or circumvents rational deliberation. A second party views it as a type of strain. A third person wants to treat it as something of a trickery.

2.6 Manipulation as the reason for bypass

Manipulation is also used to 'bypass,' 'undermine' or 'subvert' the logical deliberation of the goal. However, it is not often obvious if this argument is intended as a concept of coercion, or merely as a declaration of coercion (maybe one that describes its moral status in part). Yet let us ask that the notion of circumventing rationality through deception will serve as a concept of deception.

With at least 2 purposes, the idea that manipulative impacts bypass the capability of the target for reasonable deliberation is flattering. First, this seems fair to assume that because coercion varies from logical persuasion, this should manipulate actions by ways that do not require the cognitive capacities of the object. Second, describing aspects of influence which evidently bypass the capability of the target for rational thought as manipulative seems intuitive. For instance, suppose advertising functioned in such a manner it is commonly — though likely inaccurately — portrayed, so exposing yourself to a subtle hint imploring you to "drink coke" could impact your actions without participating in your rational deliberation mechanisms. Such an impact would seem intuitive to be a perfect indication of manipulation.

Subliminal marketing tactics — along with hypnotherapy & behavioral conditioning — are widely described as successful methods of manipulating people without their awareness and, therefore, without involving their capacity to think rationally. The efficacy of these tactics, in the famous (and often philosophical) intellect, is almost definitely wildly exaggerated. Yet if we picture them functioning as effectively as often being depicted, then they will be perfect indicators of what it could imply to suggest that deception bypasses rationality. Thus, we should consider coercion in light of bypassing moral deliberation, and recognize "bypassing reasonable deliberation" in terms of manipulating psychological processes or strategies that can produce actions without any objective feedback.

The strategy, though, poses a severe challenge. When we interpret coercion in terms of circumventing reasonable deliberation, and we using unrealistic representations of hypnosis & subliminal ads to demonstrate what it entails to override reasonable deliberation, we can place a very high standard for anything to be classified as coercion. This level may be too strong to consider all of Irving's techniques as coercion, as neither of them entirely bypasses Tonya's capacity to think rationally in the manner media manipulation, hypnosis, or compulsion is generally depicted as doing so. Indeed, as Moti Gorin reflects, manipulation also includes tactics that depend on the target's logical capacities. That is undoubtedly true of the strategies Irving uses in the examples above to influence Tonya: they all seem to be better explained as contexts of influencing Tonya's deliberation than circumventing it.

Maybe we should define deception not bypassing deliberation entirely but bypassing fair deliberation, which is also, by inserting irrational forces into the deliberative phase. So we could join Joseph Raz in believing that, unlike intimidation, exploitation does not mess with a person's choices. Rather, it perverts the manner in which an individual makes choices, shapes interest, or adopts objectives.

Treating coercion as bypassing reasonable deliberation, and instead characterizing "bypassing reasonable deliberation" as bringing non-judicial forces into deliberation, will be perfectly compatible with the finding that manipulation is counter to moral conviction. In fact, classifying "bypassing reasonable deliberation" in this context will lower the threshold to qualify as coercive for an impact.

Chapter 03: Signs of Being Manipulated

Toxic individuals are exhausting and physically wipe you down "They really need you to feel pity for them & to be accountable for all one's issues, and then they also want to solve these things. The smartest gauge is to know that how you feel upon dealing with someone — our emotional and physical responses to individuals are our biggest drivers, noting that you must consider if you're more anxious, tense, or frustrated upon seeing this human, commuting with them, or speaking to them over the phone. Such people who manipulate you for their own goodwill result in draining your mental and physical health. So as I have entailed all the possible signs of such a human being, you must beware of him or her and never let that sort of person use you for his or her own good.

3.1 Dealing with a Toxic Person

Other indications to keep a watch out are if the individual is constantly condescending, compulsively in desire, and/or unwilling to take accountability or say sorry for one's behavior.

"It may be anyone who regularly takes narcotics or alcohol, lies, or wants you to lie about them, regulates or demeans what you've been doing. A toxic man's life is always personally, emotionally, financially, physically, and/or inter-personally out of balance.

Setting Boundaries to Eliminate Manipulators

"If you feel unnoticed or misunderstood and feel manipulated or compelled to do stuff that is not even 'you,' then you may be affected by a negative human. "Toxic individuals can make you question yourself or unconsciously do something that you wouldn't normally do—you might feel a need to be fit in or cool or get approval. Every situation is different, but by influencing people to do something, toxic individuals may have a detrimental effect on others. They try to generate turmoil by negative behaviors: to use, to lie, to steal, to control, to criticize, to bully, to manipulate, to create conflict, and so on.

Effect of Toxic People on Your Life

Toxic individuals can impact all aspects of people's lives, and we are always oblivious to that. We feel sympathy for them. The myths they inflict on us are accepted and rationalized. And this, in exchange, changes how we look about our values and ourselves. Toxic individuals are happy to drive happiness down from the stuff we previously enjoyed, such as jobs, relationships, interests, and even our self-love.

3.2 Signs of Being Manipulated

Most people do not realize whether they are being deceived until it's quite late. You know when you start to do, say, or believe things that serve them, you're being exploited as contrary to you. Good people inspire you to do the brightest and motivate you. Manipulators convince people that they know what's best for you.

Then which are the warning signs – the real, clear indications if someone out there tries to manipulate us?

Always making you Guess about Them

One day they'll be absolutely delightful, and then another day, you'll wonder what you have done to get them upset. There is often nothing evident that will justify the shift in attitude-you know that there is something wrong. They may be prickly, cold, sad, cranky, or cold, and if you question them that there's something not right, the response is likely to be 'nothing' – but they'll just give you enough to make you realize that something is there. The 'just enough' could be a shuddering gasp, an eyebrow raised, a chilly shoulder. You may find yourself trying to make justifications for them when it happens or doing anything you could to keep them happy. See why that's working for them?

Quit trying to make them happy. Toxic people have long since figured out decent humans would go to exceptional measures to keep happy the individuals they value for. If your efforts to satisfy don't succeed, or if they don't last for long, then it's time to give up. Step back and return once the attitude has changed. You really aren't accountable for the emotions of someone else. If you really have executed anything to hurt someone unknowingly, ask, discuss this and apologize if need be. You don't have to conjecture at any cost.

Blame Game

It does not matter how many times a toxic individual places you in painful scenarios on purpose, and they are never going to excuse you for that. They are always finding reasons to keep you accountable for your acts.

Remember, for starters, the Xmas party where Sally the toxic person got wasted, made an embarrassment of herself and spoiled the entire night — then you blamed yourself for not controlling her alcohol consumption, suggesting that the whole thing was your fault?

Isolation

Did you notice you don't splurge time with friends and family anymore? A toxic friend will expect your undivided attention and make you feel guilty if they feel they don't give you enough of themselves.

For example, John, a toxic person, gets to control your entire time, to the large extent that he blurts out because he notices on social sites that you are trying to hang out with the other fellows and friends — that also without him. You realize then that you spend almost all of your leisure time with that kind of individual and have completely overlooked how your other mates are like. This is not nice.

Manipulative

If you feel like you are the only one that contributes to the friendship, you are probably correct. Poisonous people are capable of attempting to send out the feeling that it's something you are in debt for. Those people also have the means to take something from you or do things that upset you, and then maintain that they did it all for you. This is especially common in places of work or friendships in which power equilibrium is already out. Statements like these-' I left you with that 6 months' value of filing. I thought you would praise the encounter and the chance to know your tasks for the filing containers.' Or, 'I'm hosting a dinner party. Why don't you bring a meal here? It will give you the opportunity to exhibit your kitchen expertise. You owe no-one any of it. If it is not feeling like a courtesy, it is not.

Do Not Own their Feelings

They will behave as if the emotions are yours instead of possessing their own emotions. It is termed projection, as when they project their thoughts and feelings on you. For instance, you might have been accused of being upset with somebody who is frustrated but can't be held accountable for it. Could that be as dramatic as, "Are you all right with me? 'Or a little more straight forward, 'What's the reason for being mad at me,' or, 'why you have been down all day.' You're going to find yourself explaining and securing yourself, and often that's going to happen constantly – because it has nothing to do with you. Be absolutely clear about what is about you and what is about them. If you feel like you are defending yourself far more times previously against baseless accusations or unfitting questions, you might be projected onto that one. You don't have to clarify, validate, or fight to protect yourself as well as cope with an allegation that was misfired. Bear that in mind.

Makes you Prove Yourself to them

They will place you in a situation where you'll have to pick among them and some other thing on a regular basis – and you will always feel inclined to pick them. Poisonous people would wait till you have an involvement. Therefore the drama would then emerge. 'If you ever really cared for me, you'd be skipping your exercise lesson and spending quality time with me.' The problem with this is that never enough is enough.

Several events are deadly-unless its living or mortality, it's likely to be waiting.

Eggshells

Negative people prosper in trying to keep people on their toes and taking advantage of irrational tantrums. You never really know what kind of mood they're going to be in, so you're going to have to monitor what you're doing to them — or you're going to get 15 instant messages regarding a molehill of an issue that's resulted in a peak, including a lengthy list about all the excuses you're a bad guy, your life goes nowhere, and you are not as good enough as they are.

You may have a buddy such as Sean, a toxic person who is unable to deal with an informal meetup. And there is a whole intense moment every time you see him, he brings up a problem you've caused or needed to fix, or necessitates you in an exhausting return that pressurizes you over and tends to make you doubt oneself and one's personality.

Never Says Sorry

Before they really make an apology, they would then hide the truth, so there is no reason to argue. They're going to spin the words, alter the way it occurred and so persuasively reenact it they're going to believe their own baloney. People don't have to excuse themselves from being incorrect. And you do not need to go ahead with an apology. Just go on-without others.

Don't give up your facts, but don't carry on with the reasoning. There is really no point here. Some individuals would like to be correct more than they'd like to be delighted, and you have got better stuff to do than providing the right-combatants with fodder.

No Closure on the Issue

They are not going to pick up your phone. They will not respond to messages and emails. And among the sessions of their voice mail, you may discover oneself attempting to play the discussion or reasoning in your head again and again and again, speculating about personal life, wondering what you've done to hurt them, or if they're deceased, lively, or even just neglecting you – which can all experience this at key moments. People caring for you are not going to let you feel total crap without going to figure it out. It doesn't obviously imply that you are going to sort it out, but still, at a minimum, they're going to try. If they end up leaving you 'out there' for long sessions, take that as a signal of people's assets within the interaction.

Always trying to make you Feel Low

They're trying to pursue excuses why the interesting news is not perfect news. Examples are: For a promotion – 'Money is not so great for the type of work you are going to do.' For a vacation on the beach - 'Well weather will be hot. Do you think you would like to go? On becoming a Universe Queen- 'Well you know the Universe isn't that big, and I am sure that you're not going to have breaks.' don't let someone discourage you or reduce you to their own size. You do not need their authorization anyway - and for that issue, anybody else's.

3.3 Toxic tone- non-toxic words

The tone may be ignorant enough, and much more is conveyed in the tone. Things like, "what have you been doing today? 'Can mean something different regarding how it's said. It might mean something from 'I think you have done nothing - as normal' to 'I'm certain your day went great than mine. Mine was horrific. Just horrifying. And you haven't even noticed enough to ask.' When you ask the tone, they're going to be back with, 'What I said was what you did today,' which is true, but not really.

Irrelevant Things while Conversing

When you are attempting to solve things that are essential to you, harmful people come up with insignificant stuff from five justifications before. The issue with it is that you are attempting to argue on something you appears to have done 6 months ago prior to you understand it, also defending yourself instead of dealing with the problem. Not only has it just seemed to often end up with what you did to them.

3.4 Altering the main focus while conversing

You may be trying to fix the problem or get clarity, and before you know it, the conversation/reasoning has relocated away from the topic which was essential to you and then onto the way you talked about – whether there is a problem with your way of doing it or not. You'll see yourself justifying your attitude, your movements, your word usage, or the manner you move your belly while you take a breath – it doesn't really have to make any sense. Your original desire, whereas, has gone well on the heap of unresolved discussions that continue to get larger day by day.

Exaggeration.

'You never ...' you always'...' It's impossible to protect yourself from this abuse. Poisonous people have a habit of trying to draw on the yet another time you did not or the one you did as proof of your inadequacies. Don't let yourself into the reasoning. You are not going to win. And then you just don't have to.

Judgmental.

Quite often, we all have it wrong, and people who are harmful would then make it sure that you have got it. They are going to demean you and point the finger at self-esteem that suggests you are much less since you made an error. We are all permitted to have it mistaken now and then, but no one has the courage to stand in judgment unless we've conducted something which impacts them.

Chapter 04: Watch the Behavior of People

Everybody is distinctive; everybody has different behaviors. What would be more enjoyable than in a café, resting in a park on a bench, or on a terrace, watching other people pass by? Movements, gestures, verbal and nonverbal behavior-you will track anything.

It's interesting to watch people, see their behaviors, and look at their productivity, for many reasons. It's enjoyable, but it's very interesting as well. Realizing what inspires people, why they do what they do, and how they respond to the impacts around them would only lead to life quality enhancements. By observing such little details, you can be a better observer for the ones' who try to manipulate you in a negative way and make you do a lot for them and nothing for you in return or whenever required. I have explained many aspects regarding the behavior of humans, so be careful whenever you come across that sort of person.

4.1 People Observation

We called this "people observation" technique because it explains effectively what it actually is. Some of you might think that the language of the body is this.

Perfecting the Body Language: how to notice People's Mind Non verbally

Of course, the purpose of body language is to track and interpret the gestures, but the interpretation of people is not restricted to only that.

Observation of persons builds from the following measures:

- Political views

- Expressions on face

- Language-Conduct

- Body moves

- Way of Thought

- Correlations regarding the above

Observation of the People: why and how to do it

Let's say you haven't been so social in the past. You had recognized your issue and was wondering what your choice would be to change that.

You always needed a number of friends. Rather you might be more defined as boring. So for me to become more enjoyable and unexpected, you had to modify your own attitudes.

First, you began reading regarding body language and habits of action, which can show what people think. You got to learn many trends and tried to recognize them in others each time you would go out.

One's greatest challenge would be forcing your eyes wide open each time. You see, it was a little difficult to hold your concentration on other people's gestures, particularly at the start.

You must be cautious not to get too centered while monitoring someone else because you're going to give a weird person's impression. Also, to make associations among their motions and their phrases, you must notice what the other people have been saying.

There are two important components of body language — the main body movement (legs, hands, posture, etc.) as well as the expressions.

You could only identify basic moves at the start of the observation. When you were with someone who had performed a specific pattern at a given time, try to confirm their feelings and thoughts at that time the next moment.

You only needed to make sure their actions were relevant compared to what you had been researching.

Of course, you did not question people what they felt directly; merely informal questions.

As you are outside, keep watching the men. Reach a level at which you could concentrate on your observation at the same time and give full focus to everything else the person told.

Finally, understand that this technique had become a talent stored in the memory system of the procedures. As you practice the technique, you would then understand the process, and your subconscious will be able to understand the response of other people even if your focus is not aimed at the strategy.

That's great because you'll have a perpetual instinctive reflex regarding the persons you encounter that will always be right. In conversations with others, you should have an edge and connect easier.

Now we'll see the stages of the technique as well as how the method can be implemented in your daily life.

Body moves

Base your attention on many acts, as described earlier. There are two body language sections one called body moves and the other one as face expressions.

You have to identify some specific body language moves. Purchasing a good book associated with it will be doing the tactic.

First, learn the main body's movements, so they are easy to identify. That would be an easy starting point. Each time you are outside, strive to remember similar behavior.

Gold is what patience is. There's no purpose in reading the entire book in a week and intending to immediately implement its strategies. That is clearly not feasible.

Note, this is really a process, and it involves time and practice for the mind to learn and consciously or unconsciously utilize it. Trust your instincts, then.

Slowly you will be identifying identical patterns every day in different individuals. This situation will cause the linkages between the movement patterns and the feelings in their mind.

When you feel that all the directed movements can be detected easily, continue towards the other one. This is a good way to enhance all body motions, and eventually, you'll also be capable of detecting numerous motions and clusters of movement.

The hint is to be patient. It is a People Observation requirement.

Expressions

That's the second most popular type of body dialect. Seek to grasp the features of the hands. It can offer you far more info about other people's inner world. Yet they too are more difficult to spot.

One must confess that it really is challenging to understand trends in facial expressions. Initially, begin with the fundamentals using the same techniques as body gestures.

You will finally be able to detect various expressions. You have to take the very same measures as you appear to have done with the phase of the movements.

If you achieve a point that you can interpret other people's body language, then you can know how much you have improved your curiosity towards others. This expertise will give a competitive advantage when you interact with others.

A helpful tip to help you understand the language of your body better is to examine one's body movements and sentiments, and how the two to correlate.

This could be your initial body language practice; to interpret your body while communicating with others.

Language

Let's use psychology now. Observation of certain people's language and attitudes will give you useful knowledge regarding their personality style.

Notice when they talk to those who use a lot of "me" or "I." That shows a likely focus on one's ego. And also, glance for "defensive" expressions because a "defending" behavior may result from the accentuated ego.

People with poor self-esteem are seeking to conceal their actual selves. You can spot them by the dialect they are using.

In a fictional scenario, they usually exaggerate and stress how they might react. The reality, of course, is distinct in several cases.

Observing the words people are using, you will tell that they are healthy, evil, emotional, or just if they have psychological problems or a traumatic childhood background.

You have to relate all those characteristics to the language they use.

4.2 Watching the Behavior

Have you really sat and watched in a restaurant that has different people tables? It will not only be fascinating people observing, and it may even be analyzed into human patterns. Will an individual at one table control the discussion, raising their arms in violent hand motions while another participant sits mutely, listening to and absorbing what other person is saying? Do people at a different table appear to be drenched in a conversation that might cross on an assertion? What does all of this mean?

It is important to consider the various behavioral styles first in order to better understand the complexities in play. Most individuals are on a lifetime search for one of the following things: outcomes, communication, reliability, or factual information, and this search influences how they most of the time, behave. This doesn't imply someone who is pushed by results also doesn't appreciate interconnection or reliability; it just means that people often have one style of behavior and attitude, which appears to be more dominant than others.

Public observation of these styles can give you a pretty good idea of how particular persons are connected and how they act the way they do.

Real-world experience in a restaurant

Identifying a few of the cognitive patterns in effect can be relatively easy at a normal restaurant. The immersive individual will ask them their name when the server first welcomes them, want to know a little bit about them as well find out for how long they've been working here. They will connect with the server. They tend to talk quickly with plenty of gestures and always, first and primarily, consider the individual they are communicating to. While they're going to interact a lot and lead the discussion, they're going to be mindful of having the other individual in mind, preventing any contact that's too overt.

This is the doers that are motivated by performance. They directly communicate, are fast-paced as well as appear to have been task-oriented. Those people would typically be there on the phone pre or post buying their meals, emailing, or text attempting to increase their performance. Chances are, instead of full sentences, the messages will be given with simple sentences or bullet points because results-oriented individuals would like stuff done now. They'll definitely know just whatever they like to consume before the waitress comes to the table so they'll be eager about placing the order.

The calm person is going to be respectful and comfortable, not hasty. They're going to make the waiter chat about food offerings, regular sales, and they're going to have some informal talking. Not wanting to offend the server, that much if they know it already what they will be ordering, the consistent individual might ask the server's opinion on a meal. Communication could even start with phrases like "if you don't bother," "if it isn't too enough distress," or "I absolutely despise disrupting" with others at the table in an attempt to lighten the straightforwardness. The seekers for stabilization and doing anything in one's control not to toe the line. They are stagnantly directed than in the first 2 categories, but they target people like the engaging group. If this had been a sports betting table rather than a cafe, those would be the individuals to witness even though they prefer to keep one's emotions under control and typically show one's devilish smile.

The individual based on facts seems to be task-oriented as well as operates at a moderate speed, involved with knowing the appropriate details before continuing. This person should be one of those at the table to question what components are in any meal, side dish and sauce and how they could be replaced, changed, or omitted or not.

They are trying to ask why a certain seasoning is being used with a certain meal, and, oddly enough, they are going to be the last person to order at the table, taking their chance to create their ideal decision. Since these decisive conversationalists are far less worried about inconveniencing someone than to be wrong, those who will pose questions till they feel at ease that they have all the details they need to resolve a scenario, even if it is merely placing an order.

The discussion will probably be fascinating with those 4 personality types sitting at a table. The participatory person will significantly contribute the discussion obviously but would then do so ideologically in an attempt to earn acquaintances. The facts and results will be more straightforward and will be the candidate most likely to say stuff that could be considered rude either to the participatory or reliable person. The outcomes individual may analyze a great thing they have during a discussion, and the conspiracy theories-based individual will ask several more "why" queries to effectively understand the subject of the discussion. The queries may get annoying for the result-oriented individual who really doesn't wish to have to clarify their self in this detail.

The steady speaker will place everyone else first and notice their social skills, doing their finest at the table to listen to it and comprehend the other viewpoints. The person guided by the results would be the first one to look at their watch, curious to know when the meal will eventually be presented.

Tolerance is not a core value for the person guided by the outcomes. The participatory individual would have to contend with the desire to control the discussion. By now, the person on the basis of facts has calculated their meal's calorie count yet to show up.

Mannerisms

The results-driven people's body language is easy to identify: standing hand in pocket, going to lean forward, walking briskly, and speaking with tons and tons of the over-emphasized hand movements. Now, those who want the details and the very first time they would like to listen to it right. The participatory person tries to switch his weight a lot, and in a discussion, his hands seem to be everywhere. This person will most likely bump into someone or something when strolling, and they're too busy to look at all the individuals around. Expect plenty of large movements and facial expressions from such jovial people while having a conversation.

Body language signs for the stable person involve slouching with the hand in the pocket, strolling at such a comfortable, constant speed, and the infrequent gesture all through discussion. For the reality-driven person, body language indications include having to stand with their arms rolled up onto their chin with one hand whilst they process the information. They walk in a specific horizontal path, and when interacting, they have next to no hand gestures, rather opting to stay very restrained as they soak up the details around them.

4.3 Conflicts between different types of behavior

The individual who enjoys to actually debate larger picture notions can quickly become irritated by the person asking a lot of follow-up questions (generally the fact grabber), needing a much clearer analysis of how everything is in the manner it is. Fact seekers will ask lots of questions and feel stress unless they fully answer the questions to their satisfaction. Likewise, based on their pace, the slow and gradual individual may well be placed off (and conversely) by the outcomes thoughtful person. The person who results wants answers right now, and when it feels right, the stable individual gets around to the catchphrase. The intensity of each person will generate unease for other individuals.

When it comes to discussion, two participatory individuals at the very same table will start competing for superiority. Like two dogs struggling for alpha dog position, the other persons involved, such as the server, would find it challenging to get a word in mid-sentence.

The individual who is high in solidity would generally get along well with somebody who is social since they respect people and appreciate them. And it produces a complementary dynamic because the engaging individual likes to chat, and when the urge hits, the calm person is fully satisfied tossing into a thought.

The person focused on the evidence would possibly also get on well with a stable individual well. The steady person does not need to pose a ton of queries; they become difficult to comprehend. The truths-based individual will directly communicate, while the calm person will try to smooth the discussion with comments that render the contactless straightforward. Possibilities are, both, just like social and calm individuals, would be complimentary too.

4.4 How to Get Rid Of Manipulative People?

Some people in this world only exist and flourish because they are constantly using someone to their benefit in order to get ahead. Manipulators have the capacity to make someone else feel as if they've been supposed to pay something, but often pounce on hard-working, unselfish people who are more likely to be manipulated in their job. If you're in a situation where somebody is attempting to sway you, notice: You all are your own individual. Don't let anyone leave you feeling any differently.

4.5 Techniques

Addressing the Issue

The very first strategy for dealing with a devious person is to realize that you're being exploited, either in a job or in your private life. Such people will consider you to drift everything that you do when they need help and are extremely overwhelming in their requirements for help. They don't see your requirements in the least bit while they require you to do something, and they see their requirements as the most serious concern. If you realize co-workers or so-called mates putting their own needs ahead of yours, then immediately start to take measures to sabotage their efforts.

Inquire

Manipulators will try to even get you to do things with hardly any questions raised for them. So when you ask them a question, it changes the power balance to your side so very marginally. Ask them how or why a quest would help all interested participants, or whether they really believe it is fair what they are looking for. If they are honest, they will have to admit they are a little irrational or nonsensical. If they choose not to be truthful, you've shifted control even further to your own side, as there's no justification to do something for someone who is less than true to you.

Retain Strong

In older person clothing, manipulators just are pricks. They are preying on those they feel would not speak-up for themselves, and they think they will still get whatever they want. Manipulators, however, lose power completely once their perpetrator is standing up for their rights before them. They're so used to getting their bidding accomplished for them that they also have no clue what to do if someone disregards their requirements. They will often try and influence your decision by standing firm against such a manipulator. Don't let them do it. Only you can control yourself; compromising just once can lead to a slippery slope where aggressors are constantly victimizing you.

Use your time to benefit

Manipulators start making demands as well as enforce time limits, which cause major pressure to their perpetrators. But it's your time. If someone you know tries to take benefit of you, demands that you complete the task over a certain amount of time, inform them that you will "think about it." Doing so is as useful as completely tearing them down. In reality, going to string them along turns the table on the deceiver entirely, because they would be the ones looking for you to learn. Of course, you do not want to be the manipulator, but allowing the aggressor a dose of their very own medicine can't harm your own purpose.

Set repercussions

The demands that manipulators enforce on others who are mandates which must be fulfilled in their eyes. They're going to be doing their utmost to make it feel that you owe something to them, and have to do what they're doing. In fact, it's they who might owe you when you do such individuals this massive favor. Make that absolutely clear to those people. This particularly works if you do have other regulations that need your urgent attention. If they find that they are going to end up getting to do something in exchange for you, they would more than likely retract their demand. Although they will possibly try and find another target instead of actually finishing the work on their own, you have at least managed to get them off you.

4.6 How to notify if you are manipulated by someone — and what can you about it?

If you've ever thought that something is wrong about a close friendship or informal encounter — you're being influenced, regulated, or just even more than normal about challenging yourself — it may be deception.

Manipulation is indeed an affectively unhealthful psychological tactic utilized by individuals who are unable to directly inquire about what they need and want. Many individuals who want to exploit others attempt to dominate some.

There are several common types of coercion, varying from an emotionally manipulative girlfriend to a clingy salesperson — and certain actions are harder to recognize than others.

The telltale signs here are that you might be the focus of manipulation.

4.7 You sense obligation, guilt & fear

Manipulative action includes three factors obligation, guilt & fear. "When someone manipulates you, you're psychologically coerced to do something that you probably don't really want to do. You could feel afraid to do so, obligated to do so, or guilty of not doing so.

There are 2 prevalent manipulators: "the bully" and "the victim." To control you, an abuser leaves you feeling terrified and may use violence, threats & intimidation. The victim instills a sense of remorse in the targeted person. Typically the victim plays as hurt. And although manipulators frequently play the perpetrator, the truth is they're the ones that caused the issue.

The individual who is aimed by manipulators that act as the perpetrator often attempts to support the manipulator to restrain feeling blameworthy. Objectives of such a manipulation usually feel accountable for assisting the victim in preventing their misery by doing everything they can.

4.8 You interrogate yourself

Often, the term "gaslighting" is used to classify manipulation that causes individuals to doubt themselves, their actual fact, thoughts, or memory. A manipulative individual could twist what you're saying and make it happen to them, disrupt the dialogue, or leave you feeling like you've done something bad when you're not sure you've done it.

If you're getting gaslighted, you could perhaps feel a bogus feeling of regret or spitefulness — like you've totally failed or done something wrong, when that's not the case in reality.

Manipulators always blame. They bear no liability.

4.9 Paths are connected

If you don't get a favor just because, then it's not 'for fun and free.

If strings are attached, then there is manipulation.

One manipulator type is "Mr. Nice guy.' This person could be helpful & give other people lots of favors. It's really frustrating since you don't know that anything bad is occurring. Yet, on another side, there is indeed a string connected for any positive deed – an expectation. When you don't reach the standards of the manipulator, you'll be forced to feel ungrateful.

Indeed, one of the most popular methods of coercion is to manipulate the standards and perceptions of reciprocity

For example, a salesperson could perhaps make it look as though you should purchase a product, as he or she tried to give you an offer. A spouse in a partnership can give you flowers and then ask for something in exchange. "This strategy work because it abuses social norms," Olson says. "It's normal to return the favor favors, but we often even now feel it necessary to return the favor and comply even if somebody does one tactlessly."

4.10 You note the tactics of "door-in-the-face" & 'foot-in-the-door'

Manipulators often try out one of these tactics. The first is the strategy of foot-in-the-door, where someone begins with a simple yet rational request — such as can you spare time? —

Which then contributes to a bigger request — like I want 10 dollars for a cab. "It is commonly seen in street fraud.

The door-in-the-face tactic is the opposite — it involves somebody making a big request, refusing it, and then wanting to make a smaller request.

For example, anyone performing contract work might request you for a huge sum of cash up front, and then demand a smaller sum after you've refused. It works as the smaller request is relatively rational, despite the greater demand.

4.11 What should you do if you suspect you are being manipulated with

How you respond to manipulation mostly depends on what type of coercion you encounter.

When you believe that you, or somebody you recognize, are in a deceptive or even toxic relationship, it is recommended that you receive help by a psychiatrist or organizational assistance. A strong community group may also be of benefit. Individuals in abusive marriages need places to provide counterpoints. They're programmed to assume that the behaviors are natural. Someone has to support them break through that supposition.

Seek not to encourage the coercive actions to influence you emotionally and certain kinds of coercion.

Use the tag line, don't absorb Observe. Above everything: We are not liable for the feelings of anyone else.

Setting frontiers may also play a significant role in holding coercion at bay. People who exploit have boundaries that are crappy. Being a human, you get your own purposive background, so you ought to learn where you finish up and when the other individual starts. Manipulators also have very static or enmeshed limits, too.

It will also serve to prolong the reaction in such a manipulative scenario. For example, stay away from having a deal at first glimpse, do not make a large acquisition without thinking it through, and refrain from making major decisions about relationships the very first time they are brought up. "Sleeping upon this" is also the only means of stopping the manipulation.

Chapter 05: Emotional Manipulator

Emotional manipulators are the worst of their kind. They try to trench through all the charm and spark of your personality and have a severe impact on your mental health and well-being. I f you read through this chapter, you will get to know how an emotional manipulator drains out all of your capabilities. They will continuously degrade and belittle you to make you lose your confidence and self-esteem. Just as you encounter an emotional manipulator, he or she will try to act like your best buddy in no time and, on the other hand, will try to cut your roots from your own authentic self. They will use you in every possible way, like when they need to vent out about something bad, put the blame for something on you, and similar things. So be careful and try to save yourself for such mental leeches for yourself.

5.1 Dealing with one

We already understand what emotional manipulation sounds like. It can be highly effective. That's why it does so much for some unethical people.

An experienced emotional manipulator can destroy your self-esteem and even cause you to question your own health.

It is clear because emotional trickery could be so harmful that the recognition of it in your own life is important to you. It's not as straightforward as you would imagine since usually the emotional manipulators really are professional. They commence with artful manipulation & increase tension over the period, so steadily that you don't even recognize it is going on. Fortunately, if people realize what to search for, manipulative people are fairly easy to spot.

5.2 What the manipulator do?

They are weakening your confidence in understanding the truth.

Emotional manipulators become unbelievably talented liars. We claim that an accident did not arise because it did, so although we did not, they say they did or mentioned something. The problem is that they are so fantastic at it; you start up challenging your own well-being. Insisting that whatever triggered the question is a manifestation of the subconscious is a massively strong way out of problems.

Their acts are not in line with their terms.

Emotional manipulators can reassure you what you'd like to know, but there's another truth behind their acts. They promise their assistance, and then they behave as though the demands are totally unfair when it gets to the time to manage along. They remind you how grateful they're to meet you, and then behave as though you're a burden. That is yet another attempt to contradict your own values. As you see it, they make you doubt the truth and shape your view as to whatever is comfortable for them.

They're specialists at guilt-dumping.

Emotional manipulators become masters of leveraging the shame for their gain. When you are bringing up things that would annoy you, they will render you feel bad for discussing it. They will end up making you look guilty if you don't, for maintaining it with yourself and sulking it on. When you have to deal with emotional manipulators, anything you do is totally incorrect, and they're your fault, no matter what issues you both have.

They state the Victim's spot.

Nothing is really their responsibility when it falls to emotional manipulators. If they do — or struggle to do — it's the responsibility of someone else. Someone has had them do this — and it's you, normally. Whether you get angry or frustrated, it is your responsibility to have irrational expectations; if you get annoyed, it is your mistake to disrupt them. Emotional manipulators have little to account for.

They're too much and that too early.

If it's an intimate relationship or a company arrangement, it often appears like emotional manipulators miss a few moves.

Much too early, they share — and demand the exact thing from you.

They portray sensitivity and vulnerability, but it's a trap. The ruse is meant to make you feel "unique" to be admitted into their close sanctum, but it's also supposed to leave you feeling not just bad for themselves but also guilty for their emotions.

They are an emotional black hole.

Whoever mental manipulators believe they are geniuses to draw through certain feelings all around them. Everybody around them understands if they're in a terrible mood.

But that's not the terrible part: they're so skillful they feel it too, not just everyone is aware of their mood. This causes a propensity for individuals to feel guilty and obligated to address the manipulator's moods.

They readily decide to help — and perhaps even volunteer — then behave like a hero.

An initial eagerness to help morphs quickly into sighs, groans, and suggestions that whatever they agree to do is an enormous burden. And if you're putting a flashlight on your apprehension, they're going to turn that on you, make sure they want to support you, of course, because you're just suspicious. Target? To render you feel bad, ashamed, and perhaps even crazy.

They're just one-up to you.

No matter what issues you may have, it is worse for the emotional manipulators. By telling you how their issues are more urgent, they negate the validity of your grievances. The message? You don't have grounds to vent, just shut up and go away.

They know, and don't hesitate to hit all the buttons.

Emotional manipulators are acquainted with the vulnerable points and are able to turn the information against you. If you're uncertain about your size, they're focusing on what you're doing or whether your clothing fit; if you're concerned about a forthcoming event, they're finding out how overwhelming and condescending the participants are. Their mental sensitivity would be off the board, so they do that to exploit you, not to help you feel good.

Manipulation needs to overcome

Emotional manipulators make you insane as they're so irrational in their conduct. Let's be clear about it — their actions really go against purpose, so why encourage yourself to emotionally react to them and get pulled into the mix?

The craziest and off-base one is, the harder it will be for you to get rid of their traps. Avoid attempting to defeat them over their game. Remove yourself physically from them, and treat your experiences with them as though they were a scientific experiment (or if you like the comparison, you're the shrink). You don't have to answer to the internal chaos — only the truth.

Maintaining a distance from emotions requires awareness. If you don't realize when it is happening, you can't stop somebody from pressing your buttons. You'll find yourself often in circumstances when you need to regather and consider the right path forward. That's great, so you shouldn't be scared to buy up the time to do it.

Most individuals feel as if they have almost no solution to handle the chaos, as though they live or work with someone. That cannot be any far more from the real truth. Once you've recognized a manipulator, you'll start finding their actions more predictable and more understandable. This will empower you to act logically about where and when to come up with them, and where and when not. You can establish limits, so you're going to have to do so deliberately and proactively. If you let events happen spontaneously, you're expected to be continually involved in tough conversations. You can manage more of the confusion if you establish limits and determine where and when you'll approach a troublesome individual. The only key is to cling to the guns and maintain the firm boundaries when the individual is trying to traverse them whatever they want.

At the end

Emotional manipulators will weaken your understanding of who you are, as well as can even cause you to doubt your own mental well-being. Remember: You cannot be manipulated by anyone without your approval and participation.

5.3 Signs of both Emotional and Psychological Manipulator

What to do to identify a manipulator

Psychological coercion can be characterized as exploiting excessive authority by mental illusion and emotional abuse, with the aim of gaining strength, influence, rewards, and/or advantages at the detriment of the Victim.

Healthy social influence should be distinguished from that of psychological manipulation. Positive social impact exists in most individuals, which is part of positive interaction sharing, which takes. One human is used in psychological coercion to the advantage of another. The manipulator intentionally creates a power imbalance and misuses the perpetrator to serve its agenda.

Here is a collection of fourteen deceptive "tricks" with examples this is not intended to be an extensive list, but instead a montage of clever definitions of coercion as well as vociferous ones. Not everybody who behaves in the following ways could attempt to manipulate you purposely. Many individuals have just very bad traits. Nonetheless, in circumstances where the privileges, desires, and welfare are at risk, it is necessary to consider such behaviors.

1. Home ground advantage

The manipulative person would assert that you meet and interact in a social space in which they can exercise greater control and dominance. This can be the office, home, car, or even other areas of the manipulator in which he experiences possession and proximity (and also where you have little of these).

2. Allow your first talk to determine the foundation and search for vulnerabilities

When they foresee you many sales staff do that. They build a framework on your thought and actions by asking you basic and inquiring questions, on which they will then determine your weaknesses and strengths. Such a form of secret agenda probing may also arise on the job or in deep relationships.

3. Fact-manipulation

E.g., telling lies. Making Excuses. Two-Faced. Accusing the perpetrator of triggering victim-hood of their own. Fact-deformation. Dissemination or refusing to release important information strategically. Overstatement. Understate. One-sided bias problem.

4. Cripple you with statistics and facts

Many may like "intellectual abuse" by presuming they are the most professional and experienced in certain fields. They reap the benefits of you by enforcing on your alleged facts, statistics, and other data about which you may recognize far less. In financial and sales situations, in proficient negotiations and discussions, and also in relational and social arguments, this can occur. The manipulator intends to steer through his or her agenda more persuasively, by implying skilled strength over you. Of no real motive do certain individuals employ this strategy than to have a feeling of intellectual supremacy.

5. Cripple you with Red Tape and Procedures

Some people use red tape – documentation, protocols, legislation, and so by-laws, boards, and other obstacles to preserve their status and authority while trying to make your life harder. This tactic may often be employed to obstruct the detection of evidence and the quest for reality, mask errors and shortcomings, and prevent scrutiny.

6. Increase their voice and show emotions of negativity

During conversations, certain individuals lift their voices as a means of violent coercion. The presumption will be that you should succumb to their manipulation and offer them whatever they desire if they expressed their voice forcefully enough, or show unpleasant emotions. To increase impact, the aggressive voice is often combined with strong body gestures like excited or standing high.

7. Pessimistic surprises

Some individuals use pessimistic shocks to obtain a psychological edge and place you off stability. In a negotiating situation, this can range from low balling to an abrupt field of work that she or he would not be prepared to make its way through and execute in a certain way. The unintended negative knowledge usually arrives without caution, and you have no time to plan to combat their advance. The manipulator could request further negotiations from you to resume work with you.

8. Providing you very less or no time to choose

It is a standard selling and negotiating technique in which the manipulator places pressure on you until you're able to make a decision. By adding stress and pressure on you, you are expected on "crack" and to cede to the demands of the aggressor.

9. Pessimistic humor intended to alleviate your weak points and helplessness

Many manipulators enjoy making sarcastic comments, often masked as satire or snark, to make you feel less comfortable and less desirable. Examples might involve any wide range of remarks varying from your looks, to the older mobile phone, origin, and qualifications, to the point of fact that you stepped pretty late and short of breath in two minutes. The aggressor intends to enforce psychological supremacy on you by attempting to make you look terrible, and get you to feel awful.

10. Evaluate and belittle you consistently to leave you feeling flawed

Markedly different from the prior actions in which offensive humor is being used as a mask, here, the trickster chooses you openly. She or he holds you off-balance and preserves her supremacy by continually sidelining, ridiculing, and throwing you aside. The aggressor intentionally promotes the illusion that something is still lacking about you, so that even how many times you strive, you are deficient and never will be sufficient enough. The manipulator concentrates considerably on the pessimism without offering sincere and productive solutions or providing worthwhile solutions to help.

11. Silence

By deliberately failing to respond to your proper calls, emails, messages, or other queries, the manipulator asserts authority by having made you delay, and intends to put doubts and uncertainties in your mind. The silent persecution is a mind-game in which complete silence is utilized as leverage.

12. Pretending to Ignore

That is the traditional technique of "playing the fool." The manipulator / passive-aggressive tends to make you consider taking on what is her obligation by insinuating that she or he doesn't realize what you really want, or even what you need her to perform, and will get you to break stride. Some kids use this technique to postpone, stall and deceive older people into doing what adults do not desire to do for them. That technique is often employed by certain grown-ups because they've got someone to cover or responsibility they wish to escape.

13. Guilt persecute

Examples: Accusing someone unreasonably. Attacking a weak point of the recipient. Holding another person accountable for the achievement and satisfaction of the manipulator, or for dissatisfaction and failings.

By targeting the emotional vulnerabilities and inadequacy of the receiver, the manipulator persuades the receiver into surrendering unreasonable demands and requests.

14. The Victims

Examples: Specific problems that are exaggerated or assumed. The health conditions are misunderstood or assumed. Co-dependency. Dependencies. Intentional frailty to gain support and compassion. Acting weak, helpless, or martyred.

The intent of manipulative victimization is often to manipulate the goodwill of the receiver, the culpable conscience, the sense of obligation and duty, or the protective as well as nurturing intuition, to obtain unjustified advantages and incentives.

5.4 What should you do?

Suppose you consider yourself with somebody who maintains such strategies in a personal or business relationship, wise up. Because if you're long subjected to it, you're going to pay a huge psychological fee. Here is several thought-provoking stuff.

* It has nothing to do with you.

Collect evidence for the diagnosis and then obtain external validation not to believe or accuse it. Since you don't.

* Do not seek an explanation or a shift in behavior.

It would be awesome, but you are not going to get it. And, if you do, that's not going to be true. It's going to be anything they do and get what they want next.

* Don't try to play your own game with them.

They are going to win. They did that a long time back. From infancy, they might have been tailoring their methods, so they're good — really, very good. But let go of the urge to make the game live.

* Set health and safety restrictions.

Limits and clear edges are crucial, particularly because of family or other factors you have to preserve the relationship. You may need to have guidance from a trustworthy party outside setting boundaries to adhere to them.

* Occasionally, the exit door is the best strategy.

You should learn for better and get proficient assistance in making a verdict and a schedule if you're unsure. Don't let stuff push on for too long as your quality of life, individuality, and potential are being compromised.

* Believing things will change

You ought to hold on to that while you try to improve the condition. It is not a simple matter, but it is real. On the other side, life may be decent, fine, and genuinely wonderful. Go for it.

Chapter 06: Persuasion

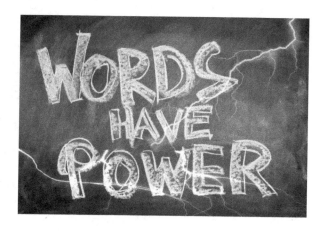

It is the process of persuading others to alter their views or to do things that you propose. People have often described persuasion as a sensitive art form, but what truly makes it quite effective? Identifying the art of persuasive communication can't just help you understand how to impact people; it could also help in a better understanding of the methods that others may utilize to modify your behaviors and beliefs. For everyday life, either you are persuading someone, or someone is persuading you. It is considered as an art due to its delicate and merging boundaries between positive and negative (dark) psychology. Through this chapter, you will be guided about all the necessary aspects of persuasion and how you can conduct it within the positive side and when it will take you to the negative side.

6.1 Persuasion- The Art

Persuasion: It is a mechanism aimed at influencing the attitude or actions of an individual (or group) towards any occurrence, idea, entity, or other individuals (s), by utilizing spoken or written words to communicate knowledge, emotions, or logic, or a variation thereof.

'Persuasion happens when faith and confidence reach risk, tolerance, belief, and security.

Over 2500 years ago, the Greeks acknowledged the fundamentals of persuasion.

Aristotle set out three 'appeals' at the core of being willing to convince someone. They are used in conjunction and provide a potent platform to convince individuals of your situation.

ETHOS

It is your integrity and reliability. When people don't value you as an individual, they certainly won't accept your thoughts – if they don't have faith in you. You have to be willing to reassure others; you possess the skills, knowledge, and, most crucially, the persona required.

LOGOS

The rational points and explanations that you bring out are as the title implies. It caters to both the intellect and rational mind. Some individuals consider statistics and numbers particularly compelling-and to some degree they are swaying many of us. Not providing a clear, coherent foundation for what we propose will hinder our capacity to convince others.

PATHOS

It's just about sentiments – the feelings that you convey as you interact with people, and the emotions that you evoke in them. You ought to capture minds and hearts-so being enthusiastic and passionate is the perfect way to achieve so. Through imaginatively incorporating tales, dramatic illustrations, and using sensory-specific vocabulary, you will relate to people's feelings to bring your compelling points to reality.

We also ought to be convincing in order to successfully put our perspectives across.

6.2 Methods to Persuade

Below are 8 methods that are well known. We certainly all know them-but are we implementing them consistently?

1. Build the trust

Aristotle understood rationality alone could not be enough to convince anyone. To be truly impactful, he recommended that demonstrating a familiar ethos, or a communal set of value systems, could be crucial first. We may not like every person, but we will trust one another!

2. Develop empathy

Aristotle goes further: he then indicated that by having pathos or an interpretation of 'what it feels like being them,' by focusing on common principles, it becomes far harder to convince others. That's why it could also be so ingenious to first hear the story of the other hand, prior we offer them ours.

3. No Exaggeration No misinformation,

Golding the claims with a slight 'poetic license' is always enticing, but remember that distortion, let alone blatant lies, does not create confidence or empathy. When only a single lie is noticed by someone, we will easily dismiss and even condemn the majority of our points. However legitimate, they might be all together.

4. Create the case from scratch

Particularly when the time is limited, it might seem appealing to first give our conclusions to others, before giving the reasons. Incorrect. For those we are seeking to persuade, don't accept our assumptions, they won't listen to our argument. They must dedicate all their resources to seeking explanations of why our findings should be false. And construct the argument from the ground up, and the final findings may well, therefore, tend to become the only reasonable, rational outcome.

5. Maintain it relevant

Many claims struggle to convince as they appeared irrelevant to persuading others. On the other hand, you ought to learn what's significant as well as relevant.

6. Just using a few strong points at a moment

In most discussions, just 2 to 3 very reasonable supporting arguments are required for a solid argument, at minimum to begin. In introducing further, while growing the probability of misunderstanding, we're not just diluting the effect of some already positive explanations we may have concentrated on. We are even giving a fortune to more captives for trivial, nit-picking discussion. At a later point, you should also announce the subordinate motives, as extra clarification if appropriate.

7. Be confident and positive

When you just don't trust in your situation, then why should someone else? Unjustified, blind faith is obviously crass; excessive confidence may indicate that the problems have not even been adequately handled. But a deficit of self-belief may imply that the situation being addressed is actually quite flimsy.

8. See and Hear Reactions

Like they say: "All who are persuaded of their intentions are always of the identical mind." And don't take marginal response as tacit approval of your ideas – they might be nothing more than 'silly impertinence!' Although some that communicate their response to your ideas very verbally, others may obviously show their quiet reaction by unintentional body language gestures, whilst others may require time to absorb what you have suggested until you can anticipate some practical answer. Don't skip out on those details.

6.3 Why is Persuasion An Art?

In order to grasp persuasion art, first, you must consider the wider meaning of it. Art is indeed a procedure and a product which includes:

• Is coherent and complex

• Is mentally rigorous

• Produces an entity or output involving a strong degree of expertise

• Carries out complicated messages

• Presents different perspectives

• Expresses deep feeling

• Is authentic

While it is obvious how all the above features relate to types of art such as drawing & performing on stage, not all refer to the persuasion art. Persuasion is not an art style in the same way as drawing or poetry but includes the precisely developed vocabulary and listening abilities or craft. Yet persuasion does integrate some of the characteristics of more conventional styles of art. It's mentally challenging, nuanced, articulate, and completely true to the personality.

6.4 What can be the Objective of persuasion?

You may ask why you would mind knowing how to convince others. You might also think of such an "art" as diabolical or malicious. The fact, though, is that, at one point or another, any productive individual has been in a place where they needed to persuade somebody of something. Of starters, most individuals have to convince an employer to recruit them prior they could start operating and making money.

Persuasion is the focus of several human ventures. Salespeople are persuading customers to purchase goods or products. Politicians are persuading voters to sign up to stand for them. Con artists are persuading individuals to opt for fraud and to waste income they do not even have. You may convince your instructor to accept a makeup exam, encourage your partner or husband to get married or convince others to support the charity drive. In general, having people doing something without any sort of convincing is incredibly tough.

Therefore, it's not even a problem that you should practice effective persuasion methods. The concern is, why have you not already done.

6.5 Factors to be considered

The technique of convincing is something that everyone should do. Understanding how to use it successfully, however, requires discipline. Any individuals seem to have the talent to get individuals to see it that way. When you consider studying frustrating, this is not the climax of life. You should know how to practice this craft, and you can. Here are a few things to remember when you attempt to persuade people about stuff:

6.6 Evaluate how simple it would be to persuade

You should begin by having an idea of how challenging it would be to succeed over the audience. Researchers have uncovered many variables that affect how simple it would be to persuade someone. You only have to obey the correct instructions and procedures.

• **Membership in a Group.**

If you are a part of a group than objectively, you are far less inclined to be persuaded by topics or proposals that run against your fellow community members' views. The group's presence and your allegiance to it help to affirm your willingness to stay with their view of the facts, even though it is completely false.

• Poor Self-Esteem.

Individuals with poor self - esteem appear statistically much easier to persuade than people with greater self - esteem. More possibly, that is because they appear to trust the views of others higher than they really value their own. The greatest obstacle you'll be posing here is assessing the self-esteem level of the individual you're attempting to convince. Often you will do so by examining aspects such as physical stance, confident tone, and dedication to the perspective of the audience.

• Aggressive Inhibition.

When you don't want to display hostility, so you are a confident speaker who is an expert in the artistry of persuasion would most easily overpower you. Even if they leave you feeling uneasy with whatever they attempt to persuade you about, lack of hostility will make it a lot effortless for them all to influence your opinions. Individuals who are just not susceptible to display aggression don't usually keep challenging what other person says.

- **Inclinations toward depression.**

Analysis suggests that unhappy individuals are more readily persuaded by adopting the opinions of somebody else than their own. It is attributed in large part, as described above, to variables like the absence of self-esteem as well as aggression. You may find, however, that some individuals who struggle from mental illness may not clearly be convinced by you but merely agree to avoid a dispute with you.

- **Insufficiency in social matters.**

Many who regard themselves as socially inferior appear to be swayed more readily. But if they are no better socially incompetent than the others, the reality that they perceive themselves in that way allows them to put the communication pressure on the individual they associate with. It makes it easy for the individual to convince them without a doubt.

Now since you understand what things to weigh when deciding to convince anyone, let's discuss the convincing method.

6.7 How to Execute Persuasion: A Procedure

Having the Introduction

An outsider can be incredibly hard to persuade about anything. Salespeople, for example, dislike cold calling as they never realize what kind of person they are working with at the receiving hand. We don't recognize their views, their interests, or that we relate to a category that rejects what / how they market. Just as significantly, the individual contacted does not recognize the seller and trust him.

Whether you can have an introduction through a relative or familiarity with one another, you stand a far greater likelihood of persuading others to consider your opinions. When you cannot receive the commencement, that can help you plan for something until you attempt to convince. It really is where strong communication and listening capabilities come in.

The Listening Value

When you first listen, you collect the details you need to formulate a personalized idea that makes sense for the person you're trying to convince. Skilled political leaders don't just arrive at your doorstep and start talking. Rather, they usually pose questions regarding the beliefs and reach a point of reference for their argument. Nice approach, right?

You establish the illusion, beyond the knowledge you obtain from listening, that you trust the other individual and support their values. They are more inclined, in turn, to shape a positive opinion towards you and respond to everything you have to suggest.

Be friendly though you disagree

It is necessary to convey agreement as much as feasible for the individual you are attempting to convince. It means you value them and therefore are neutral. Everybody needs to be conceived of as wise, and if you deny anybody's said something, they'll simply ignore you. You cannot decide to anything with anyone, of course, nor should you need to. Although you tried, you couldn't persuade the viewers to alter their stance. However, all you should do is maintain an accommodating disposition that understands the reasons for what they think and the decisions they maintain made.

Subtlety is definitive

When you can explain just what you expect people to think, so they accept it instantly, there's not much room for convincing.

Most generally, you have to convince them that your perspective is right in subtle steps. There are several various methods of persuasion to use, but those who aren't overt or transparent are the most successful. Rather, they are focused on making parallels, sharing tales, and understanding the other individual & where they are standing.

Persuading and moralizing

The art of convincing calls for persistence and dedication with the procedure. If it were merely to say, "Believe me!" not much convincing would be involved. You ought to take some time to build your points and justify your reasoning, implicitly and regularly, in an attempt to transform someone's opinion. Whether it is a short letter, the distribution will not take much time. However, if you want anything more nuanced to share, you have to be careful with the listeners to hold them engaged.

Whose summarizing is concerned?

You should pose your assumption as that of the evidence right one before bringing the case to an end. Individuals are quite effectively convinced, though, if they think they come to their best summary on a topic. They like to imply that modifying their opinions, views, or behavior is their thought. The excellent thing is, if you've explained your case to the viewers in a manner that makes sense, they'll typically believe that shift of mind was their own choice. We would also be most apt to start hanging on to the view and, most critically, acting on it.

6.7 Ethical Concerns

There are quite a few ethical conundrums to address before you decide the skill of persuasion should be practiced. Many individuals have maliciously implemented persuasion methods to hurt or benefit from others. Before you seek to persuade others to compromise with you, consider the effect that would have on them if you achieve.

Does he succeed or fail? Is it in the finest interest of them to consider what you offer?

Unnecessary interference is a legal concept that entails persuading others to behave contrary to their own independent will, without realizing the implications. It is a concern when one becomes, in a sense, incapacitated and unwilling to undertake their own choices. A caregiver, for example, could persuade an older person to shift his will and give it all to them. When you are contemplating pursuing the technique of persuasion, resisting excessive manipulation is a spiritual necessity. That could also get you clean of legal jeopardy, as well.

Falsifying Evidence

It is unethical to show falsified claims, documentation, or photographs to support the case, whether you are in litigation or posted to social media. When you intend to be fair and considerate with your persuasive process, you ought to be sure that the facts or relevant material that you send are credible and valid to the extent of your ability.

Perpetuating Scams

Those using their smoothness of argument to trick other people usually don't mind if what they do will harm others. The individuals they sometimes wind up often influencing to persuade someone of the exact idea without realizing that they were conned. So stop perpetuating other people's schemes, it's essential to keep the facts right and still be vigilant to the risk of being fooled.

And is persuasion actually positive or bad?

Like in every other art type, persuasion in & of itself is neither good nor bad. It's indeed how you utilize this art, & for what reason, that decides whether you are making a meaningful contribution to the community.

Reluctance to persuade someone may be a huge hindrance in life. You can find it challenging to get employment, buy a property, or take the next move in life. On the other side, you might notice that with any scheme posed to you, you are so quickly persuaded and fall for it. When this is the case, there are many strategies to lower the vulnerability to slipping on any slick. A psychiatrist will help you develop self-esteem, enhance coping skills, and also learn how to treat depression. Such aspects render you less prone to trickery.

Striving for guidance

You should talk with an accredited professional to receive the support you need. Online counseling is accessible, convenient, and confidential and will help you discover your concealed strengths. If you ought to practice to become quite persuasive or scrutinize certain people's convincing strategies, counseling may have a significant effect. You will know well enough on all aspects of the practice of convincing to both easily achieve what you desire and defend yourself. You deserve happiness.

6.8 Persuasion Principles

The Basics

1. Persuasion isn't manipulation

Manipulation is forceful coercion to convince someone to accept anything which is not of their own benefit. Persuasion is really the art of convincing individuals to do something that favors you, too, in their very own self-interest.

2. Persuade the one who is Persuadable

With the correct time and background, anyone may be convinced but not always in a brief period. Election strategies rely on a select group of independent voters who settle on elections. The first step in persuasion is often to recognize certain individuals who are persuasive of your point of view at a specific moment and to concentrate your energies and focus on them.

3. Timing and Context

Timing and context are fundamental building blocks in persuasion. Context provides a general norm on what is appropriate. Timing determines what we expect out of existence and from others. We have opted to marry a particular sort of individual than when we are younger because we choose to change what we desire.

4. You must be diligent in yourself to be persuading

You will never persuade someone who is not involved in what you're doing. Each of us is most involved in ourselves, & invest much of our time worrying either about health love or money. The first method of convincing is to understand how to speak about them regularly with people; once you do so, then you will still have their target interest.

General Rules

5. Compels to Reciprocation

Helping out each other live as a group is part of our social Nature. Most specifically, you will unfairly exploit reciprocity in your benefit. Through offering other people little tokens of concern, you will request even something big back in exchange, and others will gladly give.

6. Gains of Persistence

The individual who is determined to keep pushing for whatever they desire, and tries to display interest, is the most convincing in the end. Basically, the reason that many iconic personalities have influenced millions of citizens is by remaining relentless with their actions and word. Remember Abraham Lincoln, whose mother died, three sons, a sibling, his fiancé, struggled in the company and ended up losing eight different elections before ever being elected US President.

7. Sincere Compliment

Compliments impact us all so strongly, so we're more likely to trust the people we feel good about. Seek to genuinely and always congratulate others for something they are not usually complemented with, it's the absolute best thing you one can do to impress someone that cost nothing but a perfect moment of reflection.

8. Expectations Identified

Part of the convincing is about balancing the desires of others to support your decision. The CEO who aims to raise revenue by 20% and achieves a 30 % rise is praised when the same person who aims to boost by 40% and offers 35% is criticized. Persuasion is mere regarding knowing and overstretching the perceptions of others.

9. Don't Imagine

Just don't take for granted what anyone wants, always show your interest. In selling, we would always refrain from providing our products/services as we believe that some have little cash or concern. Don't think what others will or will not want, give whatever you could deliver, and end up leaving them with the decision.

10. Creating Scarcity

In comparison to the essentials of living, virtually all have monetary importance. We like stuff because that stuff is what other people like. If you want anyone to like what you do have, you've got to find the thing rare, even though it's yourself.

11. Urgency Creation

They ought to be enough to cultivate in individuals a feeling of urgency, so they want to move quickly. Unless we are not inspired sufficiently right now to do more, it is doubtful we can have any desire in the long term. In the moment, we have to convince individuals, and our most important card to use is urgency.

12. Pictures Matter

Everything we look onto is more effective than that which we hear. That could explain why pharmaceutical firms are now more open about their medications' possibly horrific adverse effects. Get your initial perception perfect. Then learn the ability to create an idea of a potential encounter you will have for someone, in other minds

13. Truth-Tell

Often the most powerful method of persuading someone is to teach them the stuff that no one else is able to reveal for themselves. The main shattering, important things that exist in our lives are to meet the harsh realities. Truth-tell beyond prejudice or bias, and you can also hear much unexpected answers from others.

14. Building Rapport

We like the individuals who we also are. It applies to our latent behaviors outside our deliberate actions. By mirroring and comparing certain typical behaviors (expression of the body, intonation, speech patterns, and so on.), you will develop a sense of connection where people become more relaxed with you and are more responsive to suggestions.

Personal Skills

15. Flexibility of Behavior

It is the individual with the most versatility who is in charge, not generally the most influential. Kids are also very convincing as they are willing and able to go through a multitude of actions to achieve what they desire (pouting, screaming, negotiating, begging, charismatic), whereas adults are left with a simple "No" answer. The greater the behavioral arsenal, the more compelling you would be.

16. Understand about Energy Transfer

Many individuals remove our strength from us while some infuse it for us. The most convincing individuals learn how to move their resources, empower and rejuvenate them, to others. Often it's as simple as eye communication, body interaction, humor, or just even constructive participation in verbal answers.

17. Clearly communicating is important

This is too difficult because you don't describe the idea or perspective to the 8th-grade student so that they can convey it to another person with ample clarification. The essence of convincing consists in simplifying it down to the heart, and expressing what it truly means to others.

18. Getting prepared helps give you the benefits

Your point of start will also be learning something about the individuals and circumstances surrounding you. Preparation meticulously enables successful convincing. For instance, in a work interview, you significantly increase the chances, becoming well proficient in the goods, services, and history of the company.

19. Detachment and Staying calm in dispute

No one is more successful when they're "On Tilt." You'll still have the most control in the circumstances with heightened tension while staying cool, relaxed, and unemotional. During the confrontation, individuals look to others who regulate their feelings and believe them to guide them through those times.

20. Using Anger Fittingly

Conflicts make certain people nervous. When you're able to intensify a problem to a greater point of stress and confrontation, many parties can, in certain situations, go back down. Using that sparingly, please should not do so from an anxious position or because of a lack of self-control. But note, for your benefit, you should use rage intentionally.

21. Certainty and Confidence

There is no such strong, entrancing, and enticing attribute as assurance. It is the one that has an unrestrained sense of certitude that will still reassure others. When you really trust what you're doing, you will still be able to inspire someone to do what is best for them, and at the same time enjoying what you wish for.

6.9 Achieving Persuasion

Most founders are so enthusiastic about their latest start-up project that after a fast launch, they can't imagine any smart person, investor, or consumer wouldn't respond quite as excitedly. They don't know they can always ruin their reputation — and potential prospects — by not engaging with zeal, answering with a sarcastic remark, or giving in too easily.

The practice of bringing people to understand it as you view them — generally named persuasion — is a crucial aspect for businessmen, so you need to sharpen the latest concept on the first day. You really have to convince the appropriate stakeholders to enter the project and develop it, the right creditors to finance it & the right consumers to purchase it.

Effective communication is really just a result of all actions and competences.

For decades, the strategy associated with prevailing over the others has also been researched and taught and tends to develop as our society evolves. Aspiring businessmen ought to research all of such things but still benefit from the positive colleagues and company advisors' tactical strategies and techniques.

1. Repetition is the secret to receiving input from individuals.

Many entrepreneurs erroneously believe their zeal would allow their message to stick out instantly over the noise of today's abundance of knowledge. Nonetheless, most individuals nowadays have built algorithms to avoid unsolicited feedback until they've experienced it in both literary and verbal medium many times.

2. Hypothesize the statement in a sense which is relevant to the recipient.

Tune the message into the circumstance or meaning of every recipient. Avoid theoretical or technical remarks which might sound like an attempt to impress or confuse the listeners with your intellect—using clear meaning proposals instead of fuzzy words such as simpler, faster, and better to utilize.

3. To explain the effect using opposing narrative scenarios.

Stories are far more compelling than pure assertions of truth. If you can specifically incorporate the recipient into the plot, then the future effect would be even greater. The force of comparison, or side-by-side analysis of performance, is an important mover of citizens to different ideas from old convictions.

4. Customize the message to suit the context of the recipient.

If you're targeting investors, collaborators, or consumers, you need to listen to the concept first and identify a particular intersection of interest. When the individual is imaginative and emotional, don't come across a rational and objective message to them. Establish a friendship, or initially do some research if you may.

5. Using mates and counsellors as pleasant introductions outlets.

Everyone is quite inclined to listen & consider new people introduced to them by those they trust in general, particularly if there is a clear related background or knowledge in that relation. Even though it takes more time to schedule such a session, it can well be worth your benefit in reputation and its effect.

6. Materialize the proposal into a project or a concept.

Customers often position more trust in something that they can reach and sound, as compared to pure words & arm-waving. What you imagine in your mind's eye is not so evident to many, particularly investors who obviously won't have the breadth of experience you serve in the product category.

7. Current signs of curiosity and stimulation from those around.

Social networking is an effective medium to check your proposal at reduced expense and risk, with tremendous ability to distribute and reinforce your content to the targeted person.

At the end, the success of company implementation is the most compelling proof of a brilliant concept to clients and associates. They would like to finance and collaborate with people interested and worthy of bringing a concept into the process of implementation. Ideally, this implies a strategy was created, with an established market plan and actual consumers that charged a full retail price with strong customer service.

Nonetheless, all entrepreneurs will begin with enthusiasm for a concept at the outset. Now comes the important part of persuading us that you think the product with the same value, persuading some to enter and support the initiative and persuading consumers to purchase it. Persuasion is by far the most valuable ability you need for success in the market, as per certain experts.

6.10 Mastering the Craft of Convincing: How to Achieve What You Want

Persuasion is indeed a difficult type of art. When attempting to convince, it's possible to be unsuccessful but still surprisingly quick to overbear. Your role as a company owner or investor is mainly to persuade. You have to convince others to come to work with you, remain in your business, follow your guide, become a client, be a friend, and write articles about you & your business and many more. In fact, there is a certain amount of convincing in almost every area of a market. When representatives fail to perfect the art of such persuasion successfully, their corporations often fail. It's hard to build a following, a client base, or a powerful team without the help of people and faith in you and your company. Thankfully, it can be practiced. Below are three ideas to help you learn the art of convincing.

1. Hear.

Listen to the employers, colleagues, and market professionals, other founders of small enterprises or businessmen. While you listen, you will understand much more, and even less when you talk. The times where you're not interacting are also the most critical moments as it lets the other individual feel that you respect their time with honesty. The easiest way to convince others is to listen to them with the mouth.

A vast amount of work confirms the idea that listening is crucial to being convincing. Bear in mind that it is important to start persuading by body language signals, including when listening.

2. Connect.

Forging a link with someone you want to convince is incredibly necessary. People are more likely to react to emotional pleas, something which dates back to the time of Aristotle. A major impact in his period, in ideology Aristotle, formed his three methods of persuasion, also defined as logos, ethos, and pathos. Aristotle found that a mixture of sentimental, logically argumentative, & plausible arguments persuaded citizens the most. In the major part, he observed that individuals were much more likely to be swayed while large rates of moral arguments (pathos) were being used. Company owners and businessmen should mimic this concept, matching the person they are talking to with the one their voice cadences, charm, and physical indicators. It establishes an intimate attachment, which helps the other individual feel that you are quite alike than you are, creating a sense of trust.

One limited yet successful approach includes integrating listening as well as communicating with the other party through mirrored words. Of starters, when the individual you're attempting to convince uses phrases like "hear" as in "I hear you," do your utmost in your dialogue to mimic the phrase, instead of utilizing certain verbs like "I see now what you say."

3. Praise

The final move in learning the art of convincing is to give sufficient attention. They start feeling insignificant and pushed aside when you just shoot individuals and their concepts down, and they tend to concentrate on nursing their offended egos rather than focusing on what you are saying. You're literally making yourself quite endearing in their eyes by rewarding the individual for the stuff you do for them or their concept. As the evidence indicates, becoming more like-able implies you are more inclined to be responded to, so you are more inclined to affect the other person. This stems from the hierarchy of needs of Abraham Maslow, a pyramid that shows the requirements that need to be fulfilled before persuading people to do specific things. People have to reach every standard before going on to the next, with the maximum being a personal accomplishment. And when you compliment an individual, they feel like they're going to hit their personal accomplishment targets, and by loving you more, they continue to believe you can support them fulfill their maximum potential. Yet be alert-do not succumb to false praise, as this will only hinder your efforts.

The biggest secret is to note that to whomever you want to convince is still a person – which many people neglect about. Consider yourself in the place of the person you're attempting to convince, and ponder about responding to other words, acts, or several other social signals. It is necessary to have the details, data, and other substantiated material. Yet don't neglect the significance of emotional and social linkages. Such relations will make the distinction between achievement & failure – and the capacity to build them.

Chapter 07: Empathy

Empathy, as I described in this chapter, is an experience that includes feeling the emotions that the other person who is your beloved or close friend is going through. You are there for that person for emotional and moral support. You can be the shoulder to cry on for someone who is dearest to you. This being the general idea of empathy, there are several other types of empathy experienced by people differently, including somatic, affective, and cognitive. I tried to make sure that with the help of this chapter, you are able to understand the true essence of empathy and how you can practice it towards your loved ones.

7.1 What is meant by empathy?

The word empathy is used to define a wide array of experiences. Emotion experts typically describe empathy as that of the ability to perceive the feelings of other individuals, combined with the potential to envision what someone would think or feel.

Contemporary scholars often distinguish between two types of empathy: "Affective empathy" alludes to the sensations as well as feelings we receive in response to the emotions of others; this may mean mirroring what that person feels, or simply getting anxious when we detect the fear or anxiety of another. "Cognitive empathy," also called "perspective collection," relates to our capacity to explore and appreciate the feelings of other individuals. Reports show a difficult time empathizing with individuals with autistic spectrum conditions.

Empathy appears to have strong origins in our bodies and minds, both in the history of our creation. We also identified basic aspects of empathy in our close relatives, in pets, & also in mice. Empathy has also been correlated with 2 distinct brain pathways, and researchers have theorized that some elements of empathy can be linked back to mirror nerve cells, neurons that shoot when we witness someone else conducting activity in very much the same way they would shoot if we perform that activity ourselves. Studies have since provided proof of a hereditary foundation for empathy, while research indicates that individuals may improve (or constrain) their innate empathy.

Getting empathy doesn't inherently imply we are going to try to support those in trouble, but it's always a crucial first move in compassionate action.

7.2 Empathy versus Sympathy

Empathy & sympathy are closely linked terms, connected by common experiences and identical situations, but not interchangeable with each other. For one aspect, sympathy is significantly ancient than empathy, truly existed for several 100 years in our dialect before its relative was adopted, and its significantly higher age is expressed in a broader meaning. Sympathy can apply to "loyalty sentiments" or "harmony or unity of behavior or consequence," concepts that are not exchanged by empathy. For situations in which the two terms differ, sympathy means expressing (or being able to share) another's emotions, whereas empathy appears to imply understanding, or being able to envision, emotions one doesn't already possess.

What's the distinction between sympathy & empathy?

Compassion, empathy, & sympathy are frequently used synonymously but not quite the same. Sympathy is a sense of kindness for somebody else, & a wish to see them happy or well off, whereas empathy implies exchanging the feelings of the other individual. Compassion is really an empathetic awareness of the emotions of an individual followed by selflessness, or a willingness to behave on behalf of another person.

7.3 Empathy

Empathy is the capacity to identify, comprehend, and express another person's thoughts and emotions, creatures, or imaginary characters. Improving empathy is essential to relationship development and caring behavior. It includes seeing the perspective of another individual, rather than only one's own, which allows for actions that emerge from inside, instead of being compelled, to be prosocial or support.

Many studies indicate empathy is now on the downside in the U.S. and other countries, results that inspire parents, colleges, and neighborhoods to endorse services that enable individuals of all ages to develop and sustain their capacity to step in someone else's shoes.

Empathy allows one to collaborate with others, create partnerships, make good decisions, & interfere when we witness someone else getting threatened. In infancy, human beings tend to exhibit symptoms of empathy, and the character grows slowly throughout childhood and into adolescence. Nonetheless, several individuals are anticipated to have more empathy towards individuals like them and may have little empathy for others outside of their families, culture, nationality, or ethnicity.

Why does Empathy matter?

Empathy lets us interact and support others, but it may have developed from an egoistic intent as other attributes: utilizing us as a "social antenna" to help identify risk. Through an evolutionary standpoint, it is important to build a conceptual picture of another individual's motive: for example, the presence of an interloper could be lethal, so cultivating responsiveness to other people's messages might be life-saving.

How can kids flourish empathy?

Babies demonstrate an intuition that the actions of humans are driven by expectations and will act upon the knowledge until they reach 18 months of age, like attempting to console an adult. More sophisticated thinking regarding the emotions of other people emerges at about the age of 5 or 6, and evidence suggests that caregivers who foster and practice empathy are growing more empathic babies.

Should we enhance our empathy?

Researchers assume that individuals will opt to develop empathy and offer priority. Those who invest more time around others who are distinct from themselves prefer to have a more empathetic view of others. Many studies show that studying novels will help to promote the desire to place yourself in others' minds. It's been shown that meditation helps to promote brain states, which enhances empathy.

What does mirror nerve cells mean?

Many neuroscientists have promoted the idea of "mirror neurons" as a potential cause of empathy. Such neurons, it is speculated, improve the capacity to show, interpret, and imitate emotional messages via facial expressions as well as other types of body language, improving empathy. However, whether mirror nerve cells really work such way in humans is a matter of ongoing research controversy, and some researchers try to find out their actuality.

Relationships and Empathy

The willingness to express empathy for a spouse, family, or acquaintance is vital to the development of successful relationships. Empathy helps one to develop connections with another human, make them know they are being understood, and imitate their feelings by speech and body language.

How does Romantic intimacy profit from empathy?

Individuals expect their spouses to empathize with them in stable relationships while confronted with difficulty or personal challenges, but the willingness to empathize, including a spouse in happy times, can be at least as significant. In one research, expressing appreciation with the positive feelings of a spouse was 5 times more effective with relationship happiness than simply empathizing with your partner's negative emotions.

Could narcissists engage in empathy?

Individuals who are in extreme narcissism, or those who possess narcissistic personality, may show empathy and even sympathy. But, that capacity only goes so far, because their own interests actually come first. Many psychologists suggest that narcissists can gain greater empathy by having deeper self-compassion that will improve their own feelings of confidence and self-assurance and encourage them to open themselves up to listen to others as well.

Empathy on the Downside

It may be helpful to place oneself in somebody else's shoes, and when it is one's automatic form of referring to anyone else, it may blind the person towards their own desires and also render them susceptible to others that might take full benefit of them.

Could you be overly empathetic, or not quite empathetic?

Individuals who consistently place other people's emotions and experiences before their own may suffer feelings of loneliness or isolation and cultivate generalized distress, even low-level depressed mood. Maniacs, on the other side, are aware of empathic precision, or accurately implying feelings and thoughts, but might have a little experiential basis for it: a real psychopath feels little empathy.

Can an individual lack empathy?

Quick respondents, humanitarian relief staff, physicians, nurses, reporters, and those whose job includes showing up to the suffering of others appear to be extremely empathetic. However, they will begin to experience the pain and grief of others they support or whose tales they report. When this "emotional debris" builds up, they can slow down, flame out, & become less inclined or able to give up.

How would you realize you're an incredibly empathetic individual?

Empaths are also described as extremely sensitive and too concentrated on the wishes of everyone else. They can profit from being alone because they consider it exhausting to stay in other person's presence. Individuals who are quite empathetic are more prone to be manipulated by deceptive persons. Thus, it is essential to establish safe limits in all interactions and to be mindful of the interaction.

7.4 Components of Empathy

Five Core Empathy Components

- Developing Others

- Political Understanding

- Understanding Others

- Built on diversity

- The Service inclination

Developing Others

Trying to develop people involves working on their desires and interests and supporting them to grow their ability to the maximum. Persons with expertise typically in this domain:

• Honor and applaud individuals for their contributions and successes, and offer positive input intended to concentrate on ways to develop.

• Offer guidance and mentoring to enable people to grow to their maximum potential.

• Have relaxing activities to enable their team to evolve.

Political Understanding

Most people interpret 'political' skills as deceptive, but 'political' in its best context implies detecting and reacting to the emotional undercurrents & power dynamics within a party.

Political knowledge may help people manage corporate partnerships efficiently, helping them to succeed where some would have struggled previously.

Understanding Others

That is perhaps what several people get by 'empathy': "sensing the emotions and experiences of others, and having a constructive involvement in their problems". Someone who does the following:

• Align with emotional signals. They hear possibly the best, and actually pay heed to non - verbal interaction, just about subconsciously getting subtle signals. Display consideration and respect the viewpoints of others.

• May support others, depending on their perception of the desires and emotions of other individuals.

These are all skills that can be established but only until you want to. Some individuals may turn off their sentimental antennae to prevent being flooded by others' feelings.

There have been, for instance, a number of controversies in the UK's health care system in which doctors and nurses have been blamed for not taking care of patients. They might have become so over-saturated to the needs of patients, without proper assistance, that they turned themselves off for paranoia of becoming incapable of handling.

Built on diversity

Taking advantage of diversity involves establishing and expanding resources across diverse groups of individuals, understanding and acknowledging that we are both taking something new to the table.

Taking advantage of diversity doesn't suggest you handle all in the same way. However, you customize the way you communicate with others to suit their desires and feelings.

Individuals with the talent value each other and connect well, irrespective of context. As a basic standard, they see variety as an advantage, recognizing that multiple teams perform a lot better than more uniform teams.

Those that are successful at embracing diversity, as they consider it, often criticize prejudice, racism, and stereotyping, building an environment that values everybody.

The Service inclination

Targeted mainly at job environments, getting a business mindset involves placing consumers' interests first and finding opportunities to boost their happiness as well as loyalty.

For consumers, individuals who bring this mindset can 'succeed.' They will truly consider the desires of consumers and would go ahead of the means to satisfy them better.

It will also represent a 'trusted consumer representative,' establishing a long-term association between client and organization. In any sector, and in any circumstance, this may develop.

There are several non-work circumstances that need us to assist others in any manner, where placing their desires in the center stage can encourage us to consider the problem differently & maybe provide more valuable assistance and support.

7.5 Compassion, Empathy and Sympathy

Compassion, empathy, and Sympathy are distinguished from each other.

Sympathy & compassion both have to do with caring for somebody: witnessing their suffering and knowing that they struggle. Compassion has carried on an aspect of practice that excludes sympathy. However, the origin of the terms remains similar.

Empathy, by comparison, is regarding experiencing certain emotions for yourself via the capacity of imagining, as though you were the person.

7.6 3 different kinds of Empathy

Three kinds of empathy have been defined by psychologists: compassionate empathy, emotional empathy, and cognitive empathy, and

• Compassionate empathy involves knowing the emotions of others and taking reasonable steps to support them.

• Cognitive empathy being a rather logical, rather than irrational, perception of someone's feelings and emotions.

• Emotional empathy which is commonly recognized as sentimental contagion, because it 'catches' someone else's emotions so that you experience them actually too.

7.7 Turning to Empathy

Empathizing towards others might not be simple, or even feasible, but we may strive for more empathetic emotions through strong social abilities and some creativity.

Research has indicated experiencing stronger interactions with one another and significantly higher well-being across life for people that can empathize.

7.8 Indications of empathy

Many indicators prove you appear being an empathetic individual:

• You just are excellent at listening to everything people have to tell.

• Many individuals show up for you to guide them.

• People speak about their issues to you sometimes.

• Tragic events sometimes make you feel overwhelmed.

• In social settings, you often feel overwhelmed or drained.

• You're seeking to help those who struggle.

• It's hard to set limits in the relations effectively with other individuals.

• Sometimes, you ponder on that what others go through.

• You're capable of picking up about how others actually feel.

• You're excellent at reminding people when they aren't rational.

• You concern profoundly about others.

Feeling a lot of empathy leaves you worried about other people's health and satisfaction. However, that also ensures you will also become weary, stressed out, or even excessively-stimulated by constantly worrying about the feelings of other people.

7.9 Other Types

There are numerous forms of empathy the individual may encounter:

• Affective empathy requires an ability to recognize and react adequately to another person's feelings. This emotional awareness may contribute to a feeling of empathy about the well-being of another individual, or it can contribute to perceptions of self-discomfort.

• Somatic empathy means getting a kind of physical response to what other person feels. Even people sense what someone else is experiencing physically. For instance, if you witness somebody feeling humiliated, you may start blushing or get a stomach ache.

• Cognitive empathy requires knowing the mental state of another person, and what they may do in reaction to the circumstance. It is linked to what researchers term the mind theory, thinking regarding what other individuals think.

Although compassion and sympathy are synonymous with empathy, substantial variations also occur. Sympathy and compassion are sometimes assumed to require somewhat of the submissive connection, whereas empathy usually requires a far more vigorous effort at understanding someone.

7.10 Uses

Certainly, humans are capable of conduct, which is narcissistic, even evil. Any local paper's quick search easily shows several insensitive, immoral, and criminal acts. The problem then is that are we not just actively engaged in those kinds of self-serving actions? What makes us feel the pain of another, and react with generosity?

There is indeed a wide range of advantages of having empathy:

• Empathy helps the creation of social relations for others. In social settings, individuals are likely to react effectively by knowing what others are experiencing & feeling. Evidence has depicted that social interactions are vital for psychological as well as physical well-being.

• Empathy for others lets you understand how to control your inner feelings. Emotional management is critical in that it helps you to control your emotions without being upset, often in periods of immense stress.

• Empathy encourages supporting habits. Not alone are you increasingly inclined to participate in supportive activities when you have concern for others, but as you show empathy, other individuals are often more inclined to support you too.

7.11 Influence

In every circumstance, not everybody feels empathy. In general, some people might be more instinctively empathetic, but people do seem to be quite empathetic towards certain individuals and less empathetic towards others.

Some of the numerous factors which play a part in this trend include:

• Previous expectations and encounters

• How individuals relate behaviors to someone else

• How individuals view one another

• What individuals accuse the other individual of their plight?

Research as well has shown that in the expression and experience of empathy, there have been gender differences, but those results are quite mixed. Females perform better on empathy measures, and research show people appear to have greater concern for cognition empathy than males.

There tend to be two key factors at the quite basic stage, which correlate to the potential to feel empathy: socialization and genetics. In fact, it breaks down nature's and nurture's age-old quantitative achievements.

Parents transfer genes that relate to the ultimate personality, which include empathy, compassion, and sympathy. On the opposite side, the family, friends, neighborhoods, and culture often socialize people. Whether individuals perceive us and how they believe towards them is also a product of the values and beliefs which were ingrained at a really early age.

7.12 Hindrances to Empathy

Some of the factors people occasionally lose empathy involve victim-blaming, cognitive biases, and dehumanization.

Victim-blaming

Many individuals end up making the fault of victim-blaming for their conditions when another individual has experienced a severe encounter. This is why perpetrators of violence are often questioned what they could have achieved better to avoid the criminal act.

This inclination comes out of the desire to focus that the universe is a just and fair place. We like to feel that they are doing everything they want and deserving what they are having — it tricks them into believing that these horrible events will never occur to them.

Cognitive biases

Sometimes, a variety of such biases affect the way individuals view the environment surrounding them. For instance, people sometimes relate weaknesses in others to inner traits, while at the same time accusing external causes of their own deficiencies.

Such biases will find it impossible to consider all of the reasons that lead to a circumstance and find it less possible for individuals to view a problem from another's viewpoint.

Dehumanization

Several actually fall perpetrator to the classic trap that individuals who are distinctive from them don't really look and act the same way they do. It is particularly normal in such situations where many persons are physically remote.

For starters, people may be less inclined to show empathy as they see news of a tragedy or war in a foreign country because they believe that others that are struggling are profoundly diverse from them.

7.13 The Science in Empathy

The word empathy was first used in 1909 as a version of the German phrase einfühlung by psychologist Edward (meaning "feeling in"). Several separate ideas for understanding empathy have been suggested.

Explanations of the Neurosciences

Studies have indicated that the way empathy is perceived plays a part in different parts of the mind. More modern theories concentrate on the mechanisms of perception and neurology that are beyond empathy. Studies clearly showed that different brain areas, including that of the frontal, cingulate cortex as well as the frontal insula, play a major role in empathy.

Evidence shows that the perception of empathy has essential neurobiological components. The stimulation of mirror neurons inside the brain has a part in the capacity to imitate and replicate the emotional reactions that individuals would have if they were in identical circumstances.

A functional MRI study often suggests that a brain region identified as the lower anterior gyrus provides a crucial role in empathy experience. Experiments have shown that individuals with trauma to this part of the brain frequently find it challenging to identify feelings expressed through expressions.

Emotional statements

Many of the first discoveries into the subject of empathy based on understanding what others know provides a range of relational interactions for individuals. The philosopher named Adam Smith claimed that, indeed, sympathy helps one to witness something we could never truly understand otherwise.

It may include feeling empathy towards actual people as well as for fictional characters. Of starters, having empathy with fictional protagonists enables us to create a variety of emotional interactions that could otherwise be unlikely.

Prosocial statements

The sociologist named Herbert Spencer stated that sympathy played an ecological role and helped the species live. Empathy refers to actions designed to improve social ties. Human beings are, of course, social animals. Tasks which often help us through our relations with people give us an advantage as well.

People become more inclined to participate in prosocial activities that help other individuals as people feel empathy. Factors like heroism & altruism often contribute to having empathy towards others.

7.14 Practical Empathy Tips

Luckily empathy is indeed a quality you can acquire and improve. There are some exercises you should do if you decide to improve on your empathy abilities:

• Have an emphasis on body gestures as well as certain non - verbal interaction

• Visualize yourself being in someone else's shoes

• strive to respect people, even though you disagree with their opinion or idea

- Focus on people to listen without disrupting

- Ask others about their life and experiences

7.15 How to establish your relationships with empathy?

Empathy is an influential power which helps to preserve the social balance and harmony. It's the process that enables people to take into account others and to interact. Empathy is indeed an essential prerequisite to affection, belonging, and loyalty. It's indeed the emotion that allows putting a stop to others' pain impossible.

Empathic individuals perceive a variety of rewards in terms of satisfaction. Empathy also facilitates selfless conduct, and it has been proven that empathy-based compassion promotes teamwork and acceptance, enhances bonds, decreases violence and judgment, and also improves physical and mental well-being.

Interestingly, evidence suggests that, while being highly empathic, happy individuals seem to be less conscious of negative feelings in others. However, in order to build greater joy in ourselves & others, it is necessary to exercise empathy, irrespective of the mood.

Practicing the primary features of empathy will help you appreciate your life more and connect with others.

Render listening to a focus

You have to know what the feeling is, so you can communicate with what somebody else is experiencing. It's important to listen — though not quite simple.

When a good pal contacts you and wants to vent out on how difficult life has become or how rough situations have been after their latest separation, the feeling in their voice typically gains your attention fairly quickly. When discussions happen despite obstacles, and with fewer apparent emotional weight, it gets harder.

Empathy starts as you set out your mind to listen for feelings. Make an attempt to note the signs that people send, which may mean what they feel.

Once it applies to understanding what other people are experiencing, your own feelings may present a major obstacle. When you're having a discussion and just focus on your own thoughts and how you can express something, you might not have been paying enough importance to what's going on the other end. The effort to listen consciously will help to improve your emotional awareness & empathy.

Share your thoughts

When you know other person's feelings, empathy firmly places you in that person's shoes. Empathy doesn't mean what you'd do in the situation; it's standing alongside yourself & spending a few moments embracing their feelings.

Some studies indicate that we are effective in this role by mirror neurons or brain circuits that fire when we feel the trigger or witness somebody else experiencing it.

Mirror nerve cells are accountable for keeping your pulse pumping as you applaud competitors racing around a field at your popular athletic event or while seeing embarrassing pitfalls in some kind of an amusing viral video causing you to cringe with discomfort.

As individuals are engulfed in the sorrow, disappointment, or anger of someone else, their sensitivity may not only stay adjacent to them and comfort them with deeper compassion, but that also sends out a signal that they're able to take on a difficult feeling, so perhaps others don't have to do it alone.

Allow yourself to be Vulnerable

Empathic involvements are indeed the two-way path. Enabling yourself to truly accept the feeling of another human will strengthen your interactions, and enabling yourself to have been open to another will improve such bonds.

You provide ways for people to understand and empathize with you by expressing feelings about your own stressful emotions, such as remorse, shame, and fear.

Becoming vulnerable provides two avenues to improve your inner empathy. Firstly, as it's mirrored back to you, knowing the importance of empathy will strengthen your dedication to becoming empathic towards others. In discussions with one another, you also find greater confidence in handling difficult emotions.

Holding on to a dialogue about traumatic feelings isn't straightforward, but if you consciously practice this skill inside yourself via taking full benefit of the moments in which you get the emotion to express, you'll be better prepared about the receiving hand.

Take a stand and propose help

If empathy resides in expressing unpleasant feelings, then joy will die. When people express intense sorrow for the victims of the catastrophic tragedy, they are moving nearer to placing themselves in the shoes of others.

But only experiencing the discomfort of someone else, though it may raise a sense of identity and being heard while shared, does not optimize the ability to promote well-being. Knowing what every individual is struggling through is getting the benefit that you can help understand what other individuals need.

As empathy implies you're accepting the feeling but not the difficult condition that gave birth to it, you're typically in a more capable position to support.

In order for empathy to become more successful and to enhance the well-being, it's really necessary to both senses another's suffering and also realize that you are in such a place to do things concerning it.

In classic research where participants observed another individual experience electrical shocks and were offered the option to support the victim by receiving the residual shocks themselves, individuals who were strong in empathy were much more inclined to walk in to help even though they might conveniently move away and no longer watch. Constructive empathy helped people to feel the discomfort of the shock they wanted to aid but not that much that they were willing to take over.

7.16 Tactics to Create Empathy

Develop empathy with the daily experience of what follows. With time, you'll find that the capacity to recognize and respond to other people's feelings is becoming better.

• **Converse with others.** Making it a practice to initiate discussions with individuals you know, even further into your everyday experiences. Pay very close interest to what an individual feels when engaged in the discussion.

• **Notice signals of body language.** This may involve tone of speech and slight energy shifts.

• **Listen by being totally focused.** Manage the disruptions as well as your own emotions that can quickly catch your mind and concentrate on being emotionally focused during the interaction.

• **Take Action.** Realize that, however insignificant, you may do something to make an impact in another's life.

7.17 Emotional vs. Cognitive Empathy

Why does Empathy Matter

Empathy helps bind people in a healing and/or helping way, turning them toward one another. When you display a genuine concern for others, the defensive capacity drops down, and optimistic energy substitutes it. That's why you will become more innovative in resolving issues."

We are always engaging and navigating the interpersonal dynamics as we enjoy our living at home and at work. We are unlikely to establish and maintain such emotional bonds because we lose empathy, contributing to tense interactions, fractured faith, loss of intimacy, and loneliness.

If we don't exercise empathy, it is difficult to fix disputes, function collaboratively, or resolve issues.

To foster interactions and further progress, our system depends on empathy. When the element of empathy is lacking, we are more isolated and less productive with creative innovations in our competitiveness and creativity. It is essential to exercise empathy in a range of relationship contexts, including those among:

- Colleagues

- Business partners

- Coworkers

- Friends

- Marriages

- Community groups

- Families

- Dating Relationships

- Siblings

The two main forms of empathy (emotional and cognitive) show how we should respond to a crisis-ridden partner or close relative. There are clear variations in empathy in both types.

Emotional empathy

- Revealing an emotional encounter

- Feeling anxiety in reaction to discomfort from another

- Feel the will to support others

- Cognitive Empathy

- Take perspective from another individual

- Imagine what it feels like in someone else's shoes

- Grasping somebody's sentiments

Emotional empathy

Picture sitting by a loved one like your kids, sibling, or good friend when they start crying. Everything they are certainly going through has an influence on us, isn't it? We might start feeling sad too. As we feel emotional empathy, we step into a mutual emotional experience from the perceptual viewpoint.

Researchers in social science Hodges & Myers discuss emotional empathy with 3 parts:

- Experiencing the very similar emotion as someone else

- Reacting to their suffering while sensing our inner discomfort

- Having compassion for others

They mention a strong connection regarding willingness and emotional empathy to support others.

In other terms, it is possible that someone who considers emotional empathy easy to do will also be motivated to support the person in need.

The value of this empathy in general health and the satisfaction of our most meaningful relationships might be convenient to see.

Cognitive Empathy

As we exercise emotional empathy, we exercise understanding that person's viewpoint. Essentially, we're thinking about what it could be like to be this individual in their case. Cognitive empathy has been called perception-taking and contributes itself to the concept of placing ourselves in the shoes of someone else.

Through cognitive empathy, you seek to tap into the concept of putting yourself in the position of someone else and having a deeper view of their life.

This might be convenient for us to take a detachment from things in times where someone we feel for is suffering, and we might see the larger picture. For instance, if a peer doesn't even get a position they've applied for, you will witness their discontent most definitely. You should still realize, though, that they really are skilled, and will hopefully quickly find a fantastic work.

On the other side, we will encounter individuals where they are as we exercise cognitive empathy, and consider why they might feel depressed or upset after not securing the job. We practice thinking what it would feel like being them at the instant, reflecting at their viewpoint on the scenario or situation.

Is it Genetic?

Evidence also found that Genetics affects the capacity to exercise empathy. Indeed, it is repeatedly demonstrated that females are more inclined to catch up on social cues & interpret feelings more effectively than males.

In a genetic testing and interpretation research, there was a particular genetic variation found as being linked to our ability to empathize, nearby the LRRN1 gene located on chromosome three, "which is a strongly active region of the brain called the striatum."

Actions in this area of our brain are thought to be linked to our capacity to experience empathy. However, there is further study to be undertaken; these results enable scientists to learn further about the links regarding genetic, developmental control, and the capacity to experience empathy.

Nurture versus nature

While genetics have proven to affect our capacity to feel empathy, there's still a lot to be said regarding our collective learning encounters. You might have heard the term "nurture versus nature" before. This concept applies to an ongoing controversy among psychologists, debating over what they think has a stronger impact on our attitudes, personalities, and circumstances.

Many studies believe genetics is the main factor, whereas others think our culture and social experiences will help us build qualities as sympathy.

Social Learning

The theory of social learning, by Albert Bandura, incorporates aspects of the theory of behavioral learning with the theory of cognition. It's proposed that by modeling and witnessing empathy from someone else, people will improve their empathy capacity.

When a child hasn't seen someone devote much consideration, energy, or importance to their emotional feelings, it's obvious how the child will possibly proceed to explore the environment as well as relationships lacking that kind of important ability. Here are a few details of what the kid will lack in:

• Understanding how to establish meaningful relations with individuals

• Experiencing someone who is empathetic while they are in distress

• Being inclined to watch someone who uses empathy and learn how it feels

• having someone show them the importance of the emotions

Empathy tends to close a distance between individual's emotions, building a bond, and mutual understanding. If we don't realize what it is like to have a common relational connection with others, it may be challenging to learn how to do it for someone.

The loss of empathy will trigger difficulties at work, in marriages, in families, and within the community.

Equilibrium

Emotional and cognitive empathy are excellent allies, and when combined with harmony, can be a great combination. This would have been a game-changer with certain interpersonal relationships to be able to consider someone's viewpoint to appreciate what it would feel like to be them, or the opportunity to approach others when they are spiritual to have a common relational experience.

When individuals feel noticed, heard, as well as acknowledged, we can do amazing things together, using both emotional and cognitive empathy. This empathic equilibrium tends to require such things as:

Excessively empathetic

As helpful and important as empathy is, so much empathy is believed to be harmful to one's mental health, well-being, and partnerships. Emotional intelligence is the foundation block of human communication. The mutual relational bond encourages one to step closer to others, console them, and provide reassurance and assistance.

Emotional empathy, however, means our body systems are reacting to the emotional responses we experience while in the other person's presence and also their emotional reaction.

If there is a healthy practice in relational empathy, we will allow room to express a relational interaction with another individual by not having our internal emotional reactions to compete with that. When our momentary emotional excitement becomes too brilliant, it can clearly impede our compassion and empathy.

Feeling emotionally misregulated may become stressful and trigger a burnt-out feeling. It actually makes you unable to exercise empathy, as it's too hard for anyone else to be involved.

Our capacity to exercise emotional empathy is a challenge to our overall health as it contributes to feelings of alienation, confusion, and an inauthentic feeling.

Not much Empathetic

There are certain individuals who are better at exercising theoretical empathy, but who have a rough time tuning in emotional empathy because these two forms of empathy operate with completely separate neural processes. It is the contrast between logical reasoning relative to emotional interpretation and point of view-taking.

There's an empathy imbalance — leaning too much on the cognitive type & not sufficiently on emotional one — our relationships with others may feel compromised. Although the individual you are seeking to support or reassure may believe you have an idea of their condition, which may definitely seem beneficial, it can end up leaving them with the feeling that they are still ignored, misunderstood or unheard of.

If there's increased cognitive empathy & not sufficient emotional empathy, the mutual relational connection with another individual is lacking. There is a simple instance of how this might sound.

Scenario 1: Empathy with Cognition

• Beloved one: "My mother has just passed away, and we've been really close."

• Person who utilizes cognitive empathy: "I'm sorry, I realize that you are depressed and that what you're going through is tough."

Scenario 2: Empathy with Emotions

• Beloved one: "My mother has just passed away, and we've been really close."

• Person who utilizes emotional empathy: "I'm sad to learn about your grandma. I know you're missing her. I'm here with you." (Might get teary or show sadness.)

In a rather simple example, if we end at cognitive empathy & don't put the piece of emotional empathy into the conversation, we will get a picture of what it would mean for any of the other individuals.

The individual accepts the deepest sympathies for the death of their mother and understands that you are attempting to provide support, but there is little ability for the individual to have an intimate connection with you. For someone in such situation, the communal emotional response can perceive quite healing and comforting.

7.18 How to Exercise Empathy

It is difficult to exercise both emotional and cognitive empathy. Both are known to be learnable by deliberate and continuous practice. The main problem of relational sensitivity is that we would definitely have to remain open and in tune with our actual emotional reactions while training.

The ability to control our own emotional pain is going to be important, but that is a thing that people will have a really hard time doing. Also, it will definitely benefit from maintaining the contrast between emotional and cognitive empathy.

Keep your views aside

Also, we don't know how often our own perceptions and values affect how individuals and circumstances are viewed. Slowing down a little to put these things apart can help concentrate on the individual with us & help us to better settle on what's going on for her or him.

Using the Imagination

Start visualizing what it feels about to be someone else when individuals interact with you. Using the pictures they send, their feelings, or their situations, and strive to put yourself in their place, only to experience what it would be like being them at these moments.

Intently listening

We often tend to hear to individuals while we are already trying to develop our defense or reply to what they say. Not just are we unwilling to comprehend what they mean, so we also skip important bits of insight, which might make us appreciate exactly what they want to convey. Grant yourself consent to switch the volume down of your own tone, and raise the sound on the voice of the other individual.

Be inquisitive

Starting from the point of interest for others when they interact with you may be useful. When you pose them questions regarding their perspectives, you let them realize that you are learning carefully, and also you intend to learn. It makes people be noticed and understood, so to exercise empathy is a good way of doing it.

Don't attempt to fix

It can be tempting for someone to want to step in and fix things while they are near someone in distress, particularly while they are feeling painful emotions. We do not relish seeing people hurt, and we mostly want to motivate them, bring joy to them, and assist them to look at the positives. This can make individuals feel unnoticed and unheard, even if you're intending to be nice.

Only offer people a way to express and understand that you don't have to "fix" them.

Chapter 08: Panic Disorder

Panic disorder and panic attacks are most commonly used in the same terms, but it is evident through the term that frequently panic attacks occurring are termed as panic disorder. There are psychological reasons behind it. If you are prone to it, then you also know the other difficulties that come along, which includes embarrassment, lower self-esteem, fear of facing people, lack of confidence. These are the outcomes that even worsen the condition and should be addressed as early as possible. A person who suffers from panic attacks is even more panicked at the thought of getting it again. In this chapter, I have provided a complete guide for you if you suffer from it or even if your close and loved one is facing it. You can help them to minimize or cope with the situation.

8.1 What is meant by panic disorder?

Panic disorder is triggered by recurrent sudden panic attacks. Panic attacks are defined by the DSM-5 as unexpected surges of extreme fear or distress peaking in minutes. Individuals with the condition experience fear of getting a panic attack. As you experience the sudden, intense terror that has no evident explanation, you might be experiencing a panic attack. You may encounter physical symptoms such as heart-racing, trouble breathing, and shaking.

The majority of people suffer a panic attack in their lifetime once or twice. The APA estimates that a panic attack will develop in 1 from every 75 individuals. Panic disorder has been described by the constant fear of yet experiencing panic attacks once you have encountered repetitive panic attacks (and even their repercussions) for at least 1 month (or even more) of prolonged worry or concern.

While the effects of this condition can be pretty daunting and terrifying, they could be controlled and strengthened with care. The most critical aspect of raising effects and enhancing the way of living is to search for care.

8.2 What is Panic Disorder Symptoms?

Panic disorder symptoms frequently begin to show up in young adults and teens below the age of 25. You might just have the panic disorder if you've had 4 or even more than that panic attacks, or if you live in constant fear of more such attacks after having experienced one.

Panic attacks cause extreme fear that unexpectedly starts, and with little warning. An episode usually lasts 10-20 minutes, but effects can persist for longer than one hour in severe situations. Everyone's perception is different, so symptoms also vary.

Common symptoms of a panic attack entail:

• Breathlessness

• Heart racing or palpitations

• nausea

• Feel like you're just gagging

• The palms or feet are numb or tingly

• light-headed

• Chills or sweating

• Afraid you would die

- Trembling and shaking

- dizziness (vertigo)

- Emotional status shifts, including a sensation of derealization (feeling unreal) or depersonalization (being disconnected from oneself)

- Pains in the chest or tightness

The panic-attack signs also appear with no apparent cause. The signs usually aren't directly proportional to the degree of risk in the area. Since such assaults cannot be anticipated, they will impact the working significantly.

Phobia of such a panic attack, as well as reminiscent of the attack, may contribute to another assault.

8.3 Questions most often asked

What gives rise to panic disorder?

This is not known what triggers the panic disorder. Studies have found that there could be a hereditary correlation of panic disorder. Panic illness is often correlated with severe life-span changes. Having to leave for college, marrying, or raising your first newborn are all big changes in life, which can cause tension and contribute to panic disorder.

Who is at risk of having a panic disorder?

While there is not a definite explanation of the origins of panic disorder, research regarding the condition may suggest that certain people are more prone to experience the illness. For fact, females are two times more likely to experience the disorder than males.

How to diagnose panic disorder?

When you have heart attack signs, you might want to receive immediate medical treatment. Many individuals who have already had a panic attack think they're experiencing a heart attack.

The medical physician will run multiple checks when in the hospital room to determine whether a cardiac condition affects any symptoms. They can conduct blood necessary to determine out certain conditions that might cause related symptoms, or check heart function with the electrocardiogram (ECG). When your conditions are not focused on an emergency, you'll be sent back to the primary medical provider.

Your primary medical doctor can conduct a psychiatric test and inquire about the symptoms. Any possible psychiatric problems should be omitted until a determination of panic illness is produced by the primary care professional.

How to tackle panic disorder?

Panic illness therapy is targeted toward raising or removing the symptoms. It is done by consulting a trained doctor and, in some instances, by avoiding medicine. Usually, CBT is utilized in recovery. This counseling helps you to alter your thinking and behavior, so you can grasp and control the fear in the attacks.

Medicinal drugs used to manage panic disorder that includes SSRIs, an antidepressant type. For panic illness, prescription SSRIs can include:

• sertraline

• paroxetine

• fluoxetine

Other drugs that are sometimes used to combat panic disorder involve:

• Benzodiazepines include diazepam or clonazepam (commonly known as tranquilizers).

• Another type of antidepressant SNRIs,

- MAOIs, another form of antidepressant uncommonly utilized owing to unusual but severe side effects

- Drugs to counter antiseizure

Beyond these therapies, there seems to be a variety of measures you should follow at home and help minimize your symptoms. As in:

- Ensure adequate sleep

- Maintain a daily schedule

- Avoids the usage of substances like caffeine

- Exercise daily

What is the long-term outlook?

Panic illness is also a chronic problem (long-term) and may be challenging to manage. Few individuals with this condition are not reacting well to the therapy. Some can have times where their symptoms are very severe, and when they have no signs and intervals. Often patients experiencing panic disorder may feel some relief from the effects of therapy.

How to avoid panic disorder?

The panic attack could not be preventable. Through restricting alcohol & substances, including caffeine and also illegal drugs, you will strive to raise the effects, though. It's always important to remember whether you develop depressive effects after a distressing incident in your life. When you're disturbed about something you witnessed or became introduced to, speak to the primary healthcare professional about the case.

8.4 Physical symptoms

Usually, panic attacks occur unexpectedly, without warning. They will hit at any moment — as you drive a taxi, deep asleep, at the supermarket, or in the midst of the business conference. You may experience panic attacks sometimes, or they can arise regularly.

There are several differences in panic attacks, but signs typically occur in minutes. Whenever the panic attack dissipates, you can feel exhausted & stressed out.

Many of the warnings or effects usually include panic attacks:

• Anxiety of defeat or mortality

• To sweat

• The imminent feeling of disaster or threat

• Feeling surreal or detached;

- Hot flashes

- Shivering or trembling

- Intense, and pounding heart rate

- Feeling pain in the chest

- Chilling

- Dizziness, faintness or light-headed

- Nausea

- Abdominal spasms

- Headache

- Shortness or stiffness of breathing in the throat

- getting cold or tingling

The hardest thing related to panic disorder is the constant anxiety that you'll get more. They can be so likely to get panic problems that you may avoid those circumstances where they can arise.

When should you consult a health care provider?

When you experience signs of panic disorder, seek medical attention as early as possible. Panic episodes are not severe, although they are extremely unpleasant. Yet panic disorders are tough to handle on their own, so without care, they will get worse.

Symptoms of a panic attack can also mimic signs of other severe health conditions, like heart attack, and it's crucial to have the primary care physician to get assessed if you're not sure what induces the signs.

8.5 Causes

What triggers panic disorders or panic attacks is not understood, but certain factors that play a role:

• Major stress

• Genes

• Several significant changes to the way areas of the brain work.

• Temperament more prone to stress, or vulnerable to harmful emotions

At first, panic attacks might arise unexpectedly and without indication, but they are typically caused by some circumstances over time.

Many researches shows that during panic attacks, the normal fight-or-flight reaction of the body to the threat is involved.

For example, if a giant bear chases you, then your body might automatically respond. Your pulse rate and respiration will intensify because the body was preparing for such a life-threatening scenario. During a panic attack, a lot of the very same symptoms take place. Yet exactly a panic attack tends to occur because there is no apparent threat present and is unclear.

8.6 Panic attacks at night: What's behind them?

Could anyone get a panic attack when they sleep?

Panic attacks at night-time can arise without any apparent cause, and you may be startled from sleep. You may feel sweating, accelerated heart rate, shaking, out of breath, panting (hyperventilation), chills or flushing, and a feeling of imminent disaster, as in a panic attack during the day. Such troubling symptoms and indications may resemble that of a cardiac arrest or another severe medical disorder. Despite panic attacks being unpleasant, they really aren't serious.

Night-time panic attacks typically only last for a few minutes; however, once you get one, it can take a little while to settle down then head back to bed. People experiencing nocturnal panic disorders often appear to experience daytime panic attacks.

Which triggers the panic disorder is not understood? Genetics, depression, and other shifts in the manner portions of the brain function may be the driving causes. In certain instances, panic-like symptoms and signs may be triggered by an underlying illness, including a sleep disturbance or thyroid imbalance. Speak to a health care provider about a problem & whether you require additional scans about a potential medical disorder.

Treatment — CBT or medications, or even both — may help avoid panic disorders and decrease their severity when they arise.

8.7 Complications/ Prevention

Complications

Panic disorders and panic attacks, left unchecked, will impact every part of your life. You may be so terrified of further panic attacks, so you exist in a perpetual state of anxiousness that destroys the quality of your reality.

Complications that may trigger or be related to panic attacks include:

• avoid social conditions

• Create common phobias, such as driving paranoia or leaving the house

• Depression, fear as well as other psychiatric ailments

• Work/school issues

• Financial issues

• Enhanced chance of suicide and/or thoughts about it

• Frequent professional treatment with dental issues as well as other medical concerns

• Drinking alcohol or using some other drug

In certain cases, a panic illness may involve agoraphobia — evirating areas or circumstances that give you fear, and if you experience a panic attack, you are fearful of being helpless to flee or get assistance. Or you can depend on someone else to travel with you to go away from home.

Prevention

There's no guaranteed way to stop panic disorder or panic attacks. Those suggestions might aid.

• Have panic attack treatment as quickly as feasible to hopefully protect symptoms from getting severe or more regular.

• Adhere to a recovery schedule to help avoid stress anxiety symptoms from occurring or worsening.

• Get daily physical exercise, which can help guard against anxiety.

8.8 What is meant by a panic attack?

Panic attack defined as an acute surge of terror that is known by its abruptness and diminishing, inactivating intensity. Your heart races, you can't relax, and you might sound like you're drowning or going insane. Many panic attacks come out of thin air, without warning, and often without a specific cause. They can also happen while you're either calm or sleeping.

The panic attack could be a one-time incident, while recurring events are encountered by others. Reoccurring panic attacks often are prompted by a particular scenario, such as speaking publicly or crossing the bridge or — especially when the scenario has previously induced by a panic attack. The paranoia-inducing condition is typically one where you feel trapped and powerless to flee, causing a fight-or-flight reaction from the body.

You can have one or multiple panic attacks while being completely safe and comfortable otherwise. Perhaps you can have panic attacks as part of another condition, such as social phobia, depression, or panic disorder. Panic disorders are curable, no matter what the source. There are techniques you should use to completely eliminate or reduce the panic symptoms, restore your confidence, and take back ownership of your life.

8.9 Panic attack or Heart Attack

Many of the panic disorder signs are physical, so several of these effects become so serious that you can believe you have a cardiac arrest. Indeed, in an effort to receive help for what they feel is a deadly medical condition, several individuals suffering from heart problems make frequent visits to the hospital or even the emergency department. Although it is necessary to rule out potential medical explanations of conditions like chest pressure, increased heart rate, or trouble breathing, fear is sometimes ignored as a probable cause — not the opposite of it.

8.10 The symptoms and signs related to panic disorder

Although certain people have only one or more panic attacks deprived of more symptoms or complications — and there is no need to fear if it is you — some individuals occur to establish panic disorder. Panic illness is characterized by frequent panic attacks, associated with major behavioral changes or intense fear about more assaults.

You might have a panic condition when you:

- Stress about next panic attack

- Behave differently due to panic attacks, like avoiding areas you've been panicked before

- Report regular, sudden panic attacks not related to a single scenario

Although a sole panic episode can last just a few mins, the experiential consequences can create a permanent impression. Once you experience a panic attack, you have a mental burden from the frequent panic attacks. The recollection of the extreme terror and fear you feel during the attacks will have a detrimental impact on your confidence and also bring significant damage to your everyday activities. In the result, this results in the following signs of panic disorder:

Anticipatory anxiety

Rather than feeling peaceful between those panic attacks and becoming your usual self, you feel tensed and anxious. This disorder derives from a perception of panic disorders in the future. Sometimes, this "terror of terror" is there, and maybe significantly impaired.

Evading phobia

You'll start avoiding other circumstances or conditions. This evasion could be focused on the assumption that a recent heart attack was triggered by the circumstance you're preventing. Or you should avoid areas where it might be impossible to flee because if you have a heart attack, support would not be available. Bringing phobic avoidance to the peak is agoraphobia.

Agoraphobic Panic Disorder

Traditionally, agoraphobia was believed to entail a dislike of large areas and public locations. Nevertheless, agoraphobia is often thought to evolve as a result of panic disorder and panic attacks. While it may grow anytime, agoraphobia typically occurs within one year of the first recurring panic attacks.

When you're agoraphobic, in a position where escaping will be impossible or humiliating, you are fearful of getting a panic attack. You may even be scared of getting a panic attack when you cannot get assistance. You continue avoiding even more conditions because of those concerns.

For starters, you might start avoiding:

- Public events, bars, or any situations where a panic attack might be humiliating.

- Many products or beverages that may induce fear, such as tobacco, sugar caffeine, or other drugs.

- Vehicles, trains, subways, and other modes of travel.

- Moving out without anyone else's company having you feel safe. You just feel secure at home in more extreme situations.

- Crowded areas like shopping centers or sports halls.

- Physical activity where panic occurs.

Origin of panic disorder and panic attacks

While the precise reasons for panic disorder and panic attacks remain unknown, there's a tendency in families to get panic attacks then pass on to the next generation. There also tends to be a link with big life changes such as college graduation and moving into practical life, marrying or starting a family. Severe stress, including a loved one's demise, divorce, or work loss, might also cause panic attacks.

Panic episodes may be attributed to psychiatric problems as well as other physical factors as well. When you have panic symptoms, it is necessary to consult a physician and inspect out the preceding possible outcomes:

- Usage of stimulants (caffeine, cocaine, and amphetamines)

- Hyperthyroidism

- Medication elimination

- Mitral valve prolapse, a mild heart condition that happens when one valve of the heart does not close properly

- Hypoglycemia (low sugar in the blood)

8.11 Self-help tips for panic attacks

Regardless of how helpless or out of reach, you can feel regarding the panic attacks, this is crucial to realize that you can do certain things to support yourself. The preceding self-help strategies to help you combat panic will make a major difference:

Get yourself an understanding about anxiety and panic.

Learning all of the fear actually will go a long distance to alleviating the anxiety. Catch up on fear, panic disorder, and the reaction to fight-or-flight encountered in the course of a panic attack. You'll learn that when you're anxious, the impulses and emotions you get are natural, so you don't go insane.

Avoid drinking alcohol and prevent using caffeine and smoking.

This may all cause panic attacks among vulnerable individuals. Try to quit the smoking habit or look for an alternate. Just be cautious of stimulant-containing drugs, such as anti-drowsy medicines and diet pills.

Know how to regulate your respiration.

Hyperventilation gives rise to several stimuli (like light-headed and chest tightness), which happen throughout the panic attack. In comparison, intense breathing will relieve the effects of panic. If you happen to feel nervous, you will settle yourself down by trying to regulate your breath. So if you learn how to regulate your breath, you are much less prone to trigger the same feelings you fear.

Practicing techniques to calm yourself.

While frequently performed practices such as yoga, meditation, and constructive muscle calming enhance the body's reaction to relief — the reverse of a stress response found in panic and anxiety. So these calming activities not only encourage healing but also enhance feelings of pleasure as well as equanimity.

Communication with friends and family.

Anxiety problems will get intense once you feel alone, so constantly reaching out to others who matter for you will help. Find opportunities to encounter other people and create supportive connections if you think you don't have someone to talk to.

Work out daily.

Exercise is a normal treatment of anxiety, so consider going around most days for at least 30 minutes (three 10-minute cycles are just as good). Rhythmic cardiovascular activity that involves both the arms and legs to move — such as walking, dancing, running, or swimming — can be particularly effective.

Get sufficiently peaceful sleep.

Poor or insufficient sleep will worsen stress, so aim to have 7 to 9 hours of peaceful sleep each night.

Intervention for panic disorder and panic attack

Treatment is the best method of professional cure to tackle agoraphobia, panic disorders, and panic attack. Even a brief recovery time will benefit.

CBT works on the thought habits and attitudes that prolong or cause your panic symptoms and lets you take a more rational approach regarding your fears. For starters, if you've panic attacks when traveling, what's the worst thing that really will happen? While you may need to pull up to the side of the lane, you really aren't prone to wreck the car or suffer a cardiac stroke. When you know that nothing completely terrible can happen, the panic encounter is less scary.

Panic disorder through exposure therapy enables you to encounter the physical symptoms of it in a safe and healthy manner, giving you the chance to learn better strategies to cope with it. You can be told to hyperventilate, move your head from left to right, or catch your breath. Such multiple activities trigger feelings that are close to panic symptoms. You would be less fearful of these inner body stimuli with increasing awareness, and experience a stronger sense of power over the panic.

Access counseling for agoraphobic fear disorder requires exposure to conditions you are scared of, which is often used in therapy. Like with exposure therapy regarding certain phobias, before the discomfort starts to go down, you experience the dreaded scenario. You know from this process that the condition isn't dangerous, and you have the power of your feelings.

8.12 Medicinal treatment for panic disorder and panic attack

A few of the indications related to the panic disorder may be temporarily controlled or reduced with medication. It doesn't clarify or cure the issue, though. In extreme cases, medication may be useful, but you must not rely just on this treatment, which is being implemented. Medicine is quite beneficial when paired with other therapies to fix the underlying reasons for panic disorder, such as lifestyle changes.

Medicines could be:

Antidepressants.

It requires a few weeks until they start working, so you'll have to start taking these on a continual basis, not just in a panic attack.

Benzodiazepines.

These are drugs that act quite rapidly (typically in under 30 to 60 min) and are anti-anxiety. Taking them in a panic attack enables immediate symptom relief. Benzodiazepines, however, are extremely addictive and have severe symptoms of withdrawal, so they must be consumed with extreme care.

8.13 How to help anyone getting a panic attack

It may be disturbing to see a relative or loved one having a panic attack. They may have abnormally rapid and slow breathing; they might get light-headed, dizzy, feel sick, sweat, tremble, or fear they're getting a cardiac arrest. Regardless of how crazy you assume their panic-stricken reaction to a circumstance is, it's crucial to note that the risk to your beloved one would feel quite real. It won't help just to tell them to settle down or mitigate their anxiety. Yet you will make them become less afraid of any potential assaults by having your beloved ride through a panic attack.

Just stay calm.

Being relaxed, calm, understanding, and non-partisan can make the stress dissipate in the beloved ones faster.

Make ones you love to focus on Breathing.

Find a peaceful spot to settle down with your buddy and then direct them to have some time of steady, deep breath.

Do physical work.

Lift and drop your arms together, or stomp your feet. This will help work out any of the tension that your beloved has.

Try to get your mate out of his or her own mind

By telling them to list five items or soothingly speaking regarding a common motive.

Motivate your beloved to reach out for support.

When the panic attack has ended, your loved one can feel ashamed to experience an attack in your presence. Convince them, and empower them to try to find support for the issue.

Chapter 9: Dark Psychology: Defined

This is the analysis of the human experience as it refers to people's psychological essence of preying on other individuals driven by immoral and/or deviant impulses that lack intent and universal theories about instinctual impulses as well as the philosophy about social science because life has the ability to damage other human beings and living things. Although this urge is suppressed or sublimated by some, and some act upon such urges. You can get a clear idea through it that everything comes with its own positives and negatives, but it depends solely on you how to use the positives of every aspect and refrain yourself from the dark side of each and everything, including the human mind. When it comes to human nature, especially inclined towards the negative side, then it can be massively destructive and brutal. I have explained different terms and terminologies so that you can assess yourself to which side you are more inclined and how you can prevent falling for the darkness and negativity.

9.1 Dark Psychology: Composition

Dark Psychology attempts to explain certain emotions, desires, beliefs, and mechanisms of cognitive thinking that contribute to aggressive actions that are antithetical towards prevailing human behavioral understandings. Dark Psychology believes that violent, deviant, and destructive activities are intentional, and 99.99% of the time contain a logical, goal-oriented purpose. There is an area inside the human mind that Dark Psychology asserts, causing certain individuals to perform atrocious actions without intent.

Dark Psychology postulates that all mankind has a reserve of malevolent purpose against others varying from mildly obtrusive and transient feelings to utter psychopathic deviant actions lacking any coherent reasoning, which is called Dark Continuum. Mitigating influences that serve as accelerators or there are attractants to reach that Dark Singularity, & where nefarious acts of an individual collapse onto the Dark

Spectrum, is what we call dark factor in terms of dark psychology.

Dark Psychology includes all that defines humans, and we actually are linked to our own dark side. The intangible disease is found in all nations, all religions, and all of mankind. Since the instant, we are birthed till the moment of death, inside us, there is darkness hiding everywhere that others have deemed evil, and some have described as immoral, deviant, and dysfunctional. Dark Psychology proposes a new conceptual framework that takes a different view of such behaviors from religious ideologies & theories of modern social science.

There are individuals who perform these same actions in Dark Psychology postulates and do so for control, wealth, sex, revenge, or some other known reason. Without a target, they perform certain horrid actions. Simplified, the goals don't explain the actions. There are men who, for the purpose of doing so, abuse and injure people. The capacity resides inside everyone. Dark Psychology believes that this mysterious potentiality is extremely elusive and much difficult to describe.

Dark Psychology believes that everyone has the capacity for threat behaviors, and this ability has links to our emotions, feelings, and experiences. We do have the ability, so just a couple of us are working on it. For one point or another, we all had ideas and fears of having to act in a harsh manner. We have always had feelings where we want to seriously harm people without remorse. Unless you're frank about yourself, you'll have to admit that you've had feelings and sound like you want to commit evil things.

Regardless of the truth, we think ourselves to be a sort of virtuous species; one might want to assume that such feelings and thoughts would not occur. Sadly, everyone here has these ideas, and thankfully, don't ever execute them. Dark Psychology suggests that there are individuals who have the same ideas, emotions, and experiences but operate upon them in an impulsive and premeditated fashion. The apparent distinction is that they operate upon them when others are only vague ideas and emotions to do so.

Dark Psychology claims that this type of predator is intentional and has certain moral, purpose-oriented drive. Psychology, religion, and philosophy, as well as other tenets, have been cogent in their efforts to describe Dark Psychology.

It is possible that most human conduct, linked to bad acts, is purposeful and purpose-oriented, yet Dark Psychology suggests that there is an environment where purposeful activity and purpose-oriented motivation tend to become nebulous. There is a spectrum in victimization in Dark Psychology spanning from perceptions to total psychopathic deviance, with little clear logic or intent. This spectrum, Black Scale, allows the Dark Psychology theory to be conceptualized.

9.2 Dark Psychology: Evolution

Dark Psychology discusses the facet of human psychology or basic human experience that enables predatory action and can even impel it. Some of the features of this behavioral pattern are its absence of apparent moral purpose, its subjectivity, and its unpredictability in certain cases. This basic human experience is believed by Dark Psychology to be special or a continuation of evolution. Let's dig at those very simple evolutionary tenets. Firstly, assume that we developed from other species and become the beacon of every animal existence at present. The human frontal lobe enabled us to be being at the pinnacle. So let us presume that just being pinnacle predators doesn't exempt us from the animal behavior and aggressive existence absolutely.

When you adhere to evolution, assuming that this is valid, so you conclude that all action corresponds to three main instincts. The three main human forces are sex, violence, and the innate desire to self-reliant. Evolution demonstrates the evolutionary principles of fittest organisms and their reproduction — we and all other types of existence function in such a way as to procreate and live. Aggression occurs to mark our territories, defend our land, and eventually earn the opportunity to procreate. It sounds logical, but in the purest context, it no doubts forms a portion of the human experience.

Our control of reasoning and interpretation has rendered us both species apex and cruelty action pinnacle. While harsh and tragic, the aggression intent matches in with the evolutionary self-preservation pattern. The lions are hunting for food, which is important for life. At times, male animals battle over death, the ruling of territories, or the desire to control. Some of these cruel and barbaric events demonstrate evolution.

As animals' prey, the weakest, smallest, or females in the group are sometimes stalked and killed. While this fact seems psychopathic, it is because of their preferred victims that their own risk of damage or death is minimized. This way, how the animal activity works and conducts. All of their barbaric, aggressive, and gruesome acts contribute to evolutionary biology, natural selection, and survival, as well as reproductive instinct. There are no aspects if Dark Psychology for the majority in life in our world. We, human beings, are the ones that embody that Dark Psychology is seeking to discover.

Once we glance at the human experience, ideas of evolution, natural selection as well as animal behavior, with their abstract premises, appear to disappear. They are the only beings on the planet today to rely on one another for the organisms' existence without the excuse of procreation. Human beings are the only species who prey unexplained desires upon us. Dark Psychology discusses the aspect of human psychology or basic human experience the enables sexual activity and can even impel it. Dark Psychology believes that there must be anything intrapsychic that drives our behavior and seems to be anti-evolutionary. They are the only creatures to kill each other for purposes other than life, health, property, or reproduction.

Over the ages, thinkers & ecclesiastical authors have sought to clarify the phenomena. And we humans have a total absence of an apparent moral motive to hurt others. Dark Psychology believes that there is an aspect of us because we are divine, fostering evil and violent behavior.

Now, then, or even in the future, there is no race of people roaming on the planet who don't hold this dark side. Dark Psychology claims that this aspect of the human experience ignores logic and meaning. It is a function of us all, and no clear cause remains.

Dark Psychology also suggests that this mysterious dimension is uncertain. Inconsistent in knowing who is behaving on such risky urges and perhaps more unexpected in the depths, others can go absolutely negated in the sense of law and order. There are men who attack, kill, torment, and assault without purpose or intent. Dark Psychology talks about behaving as a predator pursuing human targets without explicitly specified reasons of such acts. We are extremely harmful to ourselves as human beings and to any single living being. The explanations for this are numerous and efforts by Dark Psychology to investigate certain harmful aspects.

Dark Psychology captures both past theories and interpretations of violence against people.

9.3 Understanding Dark Psychology

The more individuals are willing to imagine Dark Psychology, the more they are equipped to that their risk of human predators becoming demonized. It is necessary to get at minimum a basic understanding of the Dark Psychology before continuing. 6 precepts are required to understand Dark Psychology thoroughly as follows:

1. It is a part of the psychological experience as a whole. This model has had institutional power. Both traditions, communities, as well as the individuals who live in them, preserve this aspect of human nature. Known to the most compassionate men, they have a domain of darkness, but never practice it & have reduced levels of aggressive feelings and emotions.

2. It is the analysis of the human experience, as it refers to the emotions, feelings, and beliefs of cultures linked to this inherent capacity to prey on others for simple definable motives. As all action is purposeful, goal-oriented, as well as conceptualized by core philosophy, Dark Psychology puts out

the idea that the closest an individual comes to the "dark pit" of pure darkness, the less probable, he/she has a motivating purpose. Although it is believed that pure darkness is never achieved as it is limitless, Dark Psychology believes that there are those who come near.

3. In its latent nature, Dark Psychology might also be underestimated owing to the propensity for misinterpretation into abnormal psychopathy. History is full of instances of this unconscious propensity to manifest itself as aggressive, disruptive behavior. Modern medicine and psychology describe the psychotic as an unrepentant abuser for his behavior. There is a spectrum of the seriousness of Dark Psychology asserts, spanning from perceptions and emotions of aggression to extreme victimization & abuse without rational intent or incentive.

4. On this spectrum, the intensity of Dark Psychology is not judged less or more horrific by victimization behavior but maps out a variety of inhumanity. Comparing Jeffrey Dahmer and Ted Bundy will be an easy example. Both psychopaths were extreme, and their acts were heinous. The distinction is that Dahmer performed his atrocious assassinations with an insane desire for companionship when Ted Bundy had killed

and sadistically caused suffering from utter psychopathic madness. On the Dark Spectrum, all will be higher except, Jeffrey Dahmer, maybe best interpreted by his intense delusional desire to be accepted.

5. Dark Psychology believes that any human being has a capacity for abuse. This ability is inherent in all individuals, and through intrinsic and extrinsic factors enhance the likelihood of development of this capacity through unpredictable behaviors. Such actions are intrinsically aggressive, and may also work without purpose. Dark Psychology claims psychological interpretations of such a predator-prey relationship has been distorted. Dark Psychology remains simply a psychological trait and that no other being shares it. Among other living beings, aggression, and mayhem that occurs, but mankind is the only animal that has the ability to do that without intent.

6. An awareness of Dark Psychology's root causes and influences will help enable the community to identify, treat, and potentially that the hazards implicit in its power. Learning Dark Psychology principles has a twofold purpose, which is advantageous. Second, by recognizing that we do have the capacity for harm, people with this information will

reduce the possibility about it exploding. Secondly, understanding Dark Psychology's precepts matches well with our initial biological intent of fighting to live.

We bring a mysterious dimension to all of us. This is part of nature, but it has agreed not to be known properly. Dark Psychology, an unsettling fact, encircles us, waiting eagerly to pounce.

Throughout Dark Continuum's milder aspect are the abuse of certain properties or the growing rates of brutality in virtual reality kids and teens begging for in the vacation period. Vandalism and the desire for a kid to play aggressive video games remain moderate contrasted with extreme aggression but are highlighted as concrete indicators of this common human characteristic. The overwhelming majority of mankind rejects and conceals its existence, but in many of us, the features of Dark Psychology nevertheless lurk deeply underneath the surface.

It's ubiquitous through culture, and anywhere. Many religions describe it as a force which they name Satan. Many cultures believe that demons are the culprits who trigger malicious acts. Dark Psychology has been described as a psychological disorder by the best of many civilizations or created through genetic genes handed down through the generations.

Since the dawn of documented memory, at some time throughout the day and during the night, crimes committed by one person on another exist endlessly. While macabre, it's remarkable how relatively good people would be willing to indulge in or encourage these horrors to happen.

Many of these murders show themselves across history. The holocaust now unfolding in nearby nations after WWII and religious cleansing are only a few instances. History abounds in stories of the traces about what it has created. Dark Psychology, as mentioned above, is real and very well, and needs careful examination. A theoretical structure of perception will gradually grow as you begin to investigate the principles and pillars of Dark Psychology.

9.4 Dark Continuum

It is considered to be an essential concept to understand in your journey through humanity's dark side. This Dark Continuum is an abstract mental line or distorted circles sliding down into all immoral, aggressive, deviant and sadistic activities. A Dark Continuum comprises encountered and/or dedicated ideas, emotions, beliefs, and behavior of humans. The scale varies from moderate to extreme, from intentional to unintentional.

Clearly, Dark Psychology's physical representations collapse to the Dark Continuum's right and are more intense. Dark Behavioral effects reside to a left side of the spectrum, which may be almost as damaging as violent actions. The Dark Spectrum is not a severity measure, in terms of the progression from worse to worst, but describes victimization typologies in the perceptions and behavior concerned. As this writer extends his Dark Continuum research further, you'll have a conceptually outlined line representing all aspects of Dark Psychology varying from moderate and purposeful to extreme and purposeless.

9.5 Dark factor

This factor is described as the domain, place, and ability that resides inside us all, and that is part of being human. This idea is one of the Dark Psychology's most complex words since it's so challenging to explain in the written language. In addition, it is something that causally leads to an outcome i.e., and the result has been decided by a variety of factors.

This factor is not really a mathematical calculation but a scientific phenomenon. It's a series of events encountered by an individual, which raises their likelihood of participating in predatory behavior. While the study has shown that children growing up in abusive homes may are criminals, this does not mean that all exploited children grow up to become convicted criminals. That is just one aspect of a variety of interactions and events that lead to such factors.

The number of participating elements throughout Dark Factor calculation is high. It is not the amount of factors that allow the dark factor to be serious, but the effect such interactions have on the emotional perception of an individual that renders the dark factor harmful. Many of these aspects involve genes, social relationships, emotional maturity, recognition by colleagues, contextual perception, and achievements, and interactions of progress.

9.6 Dark Singularity

This is indeed a philosophical construct related to the description of singularity just at the core of a black hole. When the idea of the Dark Singularity is highlighted, cosmology, and astronomy as a symbolism to define this idea are used. In astrophysics, it seems to be the exact center of the dark matter that is exceedingly tiny, but complex in mass further than mathematical understanding. The theory states that perhaps the singularity has become so powerful and dense, contemporary rules of science and their empirical computations become entwined.

A dark matter is the huge area of space covering that singularity, and even massive light cannot escape its grip. At the heart of all galaxies, there is an all-powerful dark hole with an incredibly narrow singularity in its core chock full of amazing energy. This Singularity, as it pertains with Dark Psychology, seems to be the center-point of Dark Psychology world. Simply stated, that Dark Singularity has been constructed of perfect darkness & absolute unadulterated malevolence. On the extreme right on the Continuum persists Dark Singularity. As well, part of human existence is indeed that singularity which no one ever achieves. The one who comes nearest to a Dark Singularity has been the evolved & intense psychotic who persecutes others with little motive or intent for his behavior.

Since all action is intentional, a Dark Singularity has become a potential endpoint never achieved. That Dark Singularity has been reached, still without arrival. The core of Dark Singularity is better described as "Predators That Attack without Purpose." The more an individual reaches near Dark Singularity, the more and more disgusting and malevolent their actions become. At almost the same point, their main tactic is less purposeful, as it is an ambiguous concept.

A philosophical and psychological tenet to understand while venturing to imagine cognitively, a Dark Singularity, would be that all action is purposive. Alfred Adler had been a change of the millennium psychologist and medical practitioner who was a colleague of Carl Jung, Sigmund Freud, and an outstanding intellectual as well.

Adler provided multiple propositions about human nature. The three most important ideas by Adler for establishing the philosophy are as follows.

Adler assumed that all actions were purposive. Since the time we are born until the moment we perish, everything we say, experience, and do has a meaning. Nothing we undertake throughout our life cycle happens clumsily. Even though his ideology could originally seem very simplified, it truly is very complicated. With this assumption in the subconscious, the reason many individuals are compassionate is that it provides that individual be so even though they reap the benefits of affirmation by their friends, family members, and society.

Children learned to be compassionate, loving, and significant contributor have greater rates of feeling welcomed and becoming part of society. For Adler, becoming aware of or a deep desire for recognition from others has been the reason for good functional conduct. Bringing his idea of all actions being intentional to the other end of the continuum, malevolent acts have a function as well.

Adler postulated that individuals who act in violent or non-accepting terms were due to a profound impression of inferiority. When people think they really aren't worthy of it or not recognized by a social community, they shift into destructive directions. If they step farther apart from their inherent desire to be component of a societal system, the farther apart they step from approaching people with compassion, reverence, and integrity. Under this precept, Dark Psychology believes that 99.99 % of all action is purposive. Including Jung and Freud, Adler contributed to the theory of Teleology.

Besides that, as people gradually grow depressed, alienated, and his social system becomes increasingly divided, the more they strike out at others in violent ways. A perfect definition and easy explanation will represent a narcissistic psychopath who becomes extremely selfish, sees pleasure in victimizing people, and deliberately taking advantage of another without regret. The definition of purposive conduct is central to the comprehension regarding Dark Psychology.

The second basic core belief Adler described core with Dark Psychology seems to be the notion of such subjective processing. Humans also have ideas, emotions, and acts, through increasing cognitive and affective conditions control behavior. Alternatively, a person's actions affect his intellect and feelings. Described as a network or what Adler considered the triad, trinity of human or a constellation, life is constituted as an interacting set of feelings, thinking, and actions. Adler applied subjective interpretation to this method of human perception.

He claimed that adolescent interactions, birth order placement, family structure, level of social recognition, and the complexities of subservience vs. dominance operated in a way to establish a person's subjective perception and pattern of communicating with his environment.

The simplest way to explain subjective sorting, as well as the perception structure, is by envisioning a pair of shades. Such shaded eye-wear filter light & prevent your eyes from sun's damaging rays. Your eyes portray true reality, as well as the sunglasses, portray your filtering method trying to distort the truth of the brutal sunlight. Hence, your "perceptual shades "distort, filter, and change how you perceive details and react accordingly.

That is how subjective reasoning functions, although extended to the actual experience. Truth exists and happens each second around us. Subjective analysis filters our perception to both secure and defends us from what we believe might be contrary signaled to the purposive objectives. When the person evolves in an atmosphere that he sees being aware of, contributing to, & acknowledged, his contextual perception filtering system makes feedback that is far more precise. A person socially conditioned in what he considers as a negative environment, their emotional perception is skewed and blurred with narcissism and selfishness.

About Dark Psychology, its aim is to presume that almost all individuals filter their environment through subjective analysis. Some individuals that are mean, threatening, or disrespectful are sporting a set of hypothetical shades that are shortsighted and blurred. Such people believe others are just out to hurt them and switch to attack or exploit them first. A contextual interpretation distorts social dignity, benevolent actions, and selflessness. Acts of compassion are alien encounters or used to exploit their social climate driven by a narcissistic core philosophy.

Adler's third tenet essential to knowing Dark Psychology is the philosophy of Social Interest. This third tenet, posited by Adler, has been the accumulation of beliefs, emotions, and feelings converted into benign behaviors. Clearly put, the more an individual feels embraced by everyone, the further they feel like part of, as well as the greater feeling of involvement explicitly relates to an individual's Social Interest. Individuals with elevated Social Interest become naturally loving, selfless, generous, and responsive. Each of these characteristics related to Social Interest-only solidifies their emotional thinking to be optimistic and caring. Elevated Social Interest implies reduced Dark Psychology influence.

Despite that, all humans possess Dark Factor inside; the individual with elevated Social Interest holds the Dark Factor suppressed. The lesser your Social Interest, there is much greater the chance the Dark Factor arises. If an individual is depressed, doesn't really feel like part of, will not encounter a sense of belonging, and interprets his environment as segregating, he would be at a greater risk for experiencing unhealthy violent reactions. Associated with Adler and propositional behavior, qualitative processing as well as Social Interest have always been central to comprehending Dark Psychology.

If you have an understanding of Dark Psychology, then you should also have the opportunity to judge certain people's behavior as being extremely harmful.

Also, Dark Psychology encompasses both immoral and deviant actions perpetrated against innocent individuals. While several viewers are fascinated by the topic of serial murderer & psychopath, the overwhelming number of predators seeking human victims are not involved in the assassination or sexual perversions.

Dark Psychology believes what exists inside both of us is a hidden source of aggressive, destructive force. Everything life rests anywhere along that Dark Continuum accompanied by much falling in the range of vague, weak, and often brief emotions and slight shortfalls. The truth, however, is Dark

Psychology is a common trend, so there is no doubt that all humans, at points in life, have had at least feelings of pure aggression and predatory illusions.

The irony that the overwhelming majority of mankind has never operated upon such feelings. The explanation is we've had a weak Dark Factor relative to the monsters. To them, the Dark Factor becomes elevated, causing them to step in a path of what others perceive as evil.

Dark Psychology, as well as the human attacker, have a deeply skewed visual selection system. To them, this is no more about being humane and loving. Their subjective thinking paints all of their feelings, impulses, and experiences with darkness and poison.

For any stage in the creation of the human abuser, he/she initiates his emotions & feelings as well as continues on the long track to what modern criminologist term psychopathy. Over time, their emotional, cognitive system is removed from feeling regret. They tend to understand that the victim-hood of someone is earned by the person who is too ignorant to secure oneself.

Considering that a significant majority of human existence involves societal recognition, the abuser somehow ventures into the environment where the Dark Factor is a powerful factor fueling an appetite for the degradation of another. When affected by the domain of psychopathy, the person has reached the end of the road. Quite like light cannot flee a bottomless pit, the human intruder cannot avoid the journey into Dark Singularity. Interviews performed by forensic investigators and investigative psychologists of imprisoned infamous psychopaths have confirmed the hypothesis of exponential development into Dark Singularity.

And not just psychopaths have disclosed a feeling of having a sensation that their bad deeds increase in duration, but even their awareness of functioning as predator carries on an enticing nature. Considering cosmology yet again as a model regarding Dark Psychology, as more matter enters that black hole, the further mass speeds up and will never turn free through the black hole's incredible gravity.

Conversations of psychopaths nearly perfectly mirror this fundamental rule in astrophysics.

As society ventures forward towards what is known as the Modern Era riddled with cyberspace & new media, Dark

Psychology & its effects on mankind can be examined at greater levels. Despite the cloak of protection cyberspace provides to humans, the problem remains whether the dark forces residing within every one of us would know there is a world of complete freedom named as the digital world.

Chapter 10: Dark Side of Human Consciousness Concept

Dark Psychology involves the science of the human experience as it refers to people's psychological intent by preying on others. Humanity, as a whole, has the ability to victimize certain human beings & living things. Although this urge is suppressed or sublimated by others, others act upon such urges. Dark Psychology attempts to explain the thoughts, feelings, and beliefs that contribute to the behavior of human predators. Dark Psychology believes that development is intentional, and 99.99 % of the time contains a logical, goal-oriented purpose. Within Dark Psychology, the remaining 0.01

% is the violent victimization of someone without purposeful aim or fairly described by natural theory or moral ideology. So beware of yourself and someone around you possessing such qualities to stay away from the dark side of the human mind. I have described in this chapter the other terms used for violent or dark psych in order for you to keep yourself safe and sound.

10.1 iPredator

iPredators and other actions of robbery, brutality, and harassment would become, if not eliminated, a worldwide trend and social problem over the next era. iPredator divisions cover cyber sexual predators, cyber-bullies, cyber-threats, cyber-stalkers, cyber-criminals, and cyber warfare-engaged in religious/political fanatics. Just like Dark Psychology considers all deviant/criminal conduct on a spectrum of seriousness and purposeful motive, iPredator's idea fits the same structure but includes violence, harassment, and cyber victimization through ICT. The iPredator description reads as follows:

A human, community, or country engaged, explicitly or indirectly, in the abuse, victimization, intimidation, harassment, robbery, or dismissal of others utilizing ICT. The iPredators are motivated by deviant impulses, urges for perceptual distortions, dominance, and influence, religious fanaticism, revenge, political repression, mental disorder, social recognition, or psychological and financial benefit. iPredators can be of every age or ethnicity and are not protected by financial status, ethnic, spiritual, or national identity. iPredator is indeed a global concept used to identify those who use ICT to indulge in violent, manipulative, deviant, or harmful behaviors. Core to the concept is the idea that psychopathological categories foreign to humanity are Internet Age criminals, psychos, and extensively disturbed.

If the perpetrator is a cyber-harasser, cyber-stalker, online sexual abuser, cyber-bully, cyber-terrorist, cyber-criminal, internet troll, digital child porn user/distributor, or engaging in internet vilification or malicious web fraud, they come under the context of iPredator. The three parameters employed to identify an iPredator are:

• A self-consciousness about hurting someone, consciously or implicitly, through utilizing ICTs.

• Use of ICT for collecting, sharing, and revealing hazardous details.

- A broad concept of Cyber-stealth used to partake in illegal or deviant behavior or profile, recognize, track, stalk, and aim.

Such as human predators before the Internet Age, iPredators depend on the wide range of benefits that ICT provides. Such benefits involve the sharing of information across large distances, the pace of transmission of information, and the almost unlimited exposure to accessible data. Intentionally malevolent, iPredators typically manipulate us in the hypothetical and fictional technological world defined as cyberspace, utilizing ICT. While the internet obviously provides privacy to all ICT consumers, iPredators deliberately develop online identities & diversionary strategies to stay unidentified and undetected if they really want.

Cyber stealth, an iPredator sub-tenet, is a clandestine approach through which iPredators aim to create and preserve full secrecy when engaged in ICT operations, plotting their next attack, testing new monitoring techniques or studying their next target's social media. Consistent with the idea of cyber-stealth is IVI, iPredator's IVI is their capacity to detect ODDOR, offline and online shortcomings, psychological vulnerabilities, computational limits, raising their effectiveness with limited repercussions in a cyber-attack.

10.2 Arsonist

That is an individual with an excessive passion for lighting fire. Such people also have a background of growth loaded with sexual and physical violence. Popular in serial arsonists has been the affection for being loners, with few friends, and are utterly intrigued by the lighting of fire and devastation. Serial arsonists become strongly ritualistic & continue to display patterned attitudes about their fire-setting methodologies.

Worried about the setting of a fire, Arsonists frequently brag & focus about how to design their episodes of fire setting. Many arsonists feel sexual arousal until their aim is put to ablaze and continue with masturbation as they watch. The prolific arsonist takes satisfaction in his acts, given their obsessive and ritualistic habits.

10.3 Necrophilia

Necrologies, thanatophilia, and necrophilia all describe the very same type of individual being disordered. There are men who possess a sexual desire with corpses, and they actually exist. Necrophilia is also termed as paraphilia. A paraphilia-medical word has been using to define a person's sexual excitement and concern with objects, situations, or persons which are not component of subjective stimuli and may trigger serious issue or distress in such person. A paraphilia of a Necrophile is, therefore, sexual excitement by a deceased human or an object.

Experts that have collected necrophile profiles reveal that they have immense difficulty undergoing an ability to be sexual with somebody. Sexual activity with the deceased sounds secure and safe to these individuals, instead of sexual interaction with just a human being. Necrophiles, in the association of a dead, have disclosed in discussions feeling a wonderful experience of the rule. A feel of belonging does become inferior to the perception of control primarily needed.

10.4 Serial Killer

The serial killer is indeed a real human murderer, usually described as one that kills three or even more victims in a 30-day or longer duration. Interviews of several serial killers showed they undergo a time of cooling off in each killing. The cooling off phase of a serial killer is a mental refractory era, during which they become briefly satiated by a desire to inflict harm to others.

Researchers of Criminal Psychology have speculated that their motive for violence is the creation of personal pleasure, only obtained by abuse. Such people have a sense of empowerment mixed with egotistical control when they kill. The encounter for them provides such satisfaction that once again, they are wanton to reach the feeling of freedom and pleasure.

During the process of their killings, sexual harassment, abuse, embarrassment, and terror were sometimes included. In addition to rage, anger, recognition seeking, enjoyment finding & monetary benefit, there are other motives. Serial murderers also show common tendencies in their choosing of hostages, how they assassinate their victims, and methods of disposing of the corpse. Criminal analysts specializing in conduct research conclude the serial murderers have a pattern of significant mental, behavioral, and social dysfunction. Even if not cumulative, serial murderers appear to be lonely people who encounter practical partnership problems.

Four descriptions of criminals and offender classes performing coercive and/or aggressive, bizarre crimes bearing the shared connection of profound psychiatric disorders and skewed worldviews are presented above. Those dangerous structures of psychological and/or identity that may grow rapidly during their being transcend explanation. How do these humans become criminals, how might they act in their daily lives & socialize? Such short portraits speak volumes regarding the human condition's morbid reality. Besides having moderate to extreme psychopathology, they are both visual loners accompanied by deep-seated powers that control their decision-making ability.

The professional arsonist does not attack other individuals or derive pleasure by becoming a man predator, as would the serial murderer, but from the fire environment, he truly feels happiness and elation. He experiences a perception of pride, as well as pleasure, from the destruction he has created. The incidents of fire setup are particularly risky provided that he may injure anyone, but the main tactic is not the aim of causing suffering or bodily damage.

The main reward for the prolific arsonist is his feeling of confidence and warped understanding of carrying in a great feat of brilliance. At times his perverted feeling of pride causes him to become physically stimulated, and masturbation continues. The action of the arsonist is reprehensible, immoral, and hazardous but does not usually include premeditated assassination. We linger inside an ocean of hellish madness.

Whereas the Necrophile does not inflict harm to another human or victimize others, its acts are exceedingly bizarre and ignore any form of reasoning. The desire for supposed dominance of the Necrophile is so subtle that it eventually creates a physical appetite towards a corpse. Think about what it would feel for him to encounter. A dead body that is expressionless as well as devoid of blood renders him sexually aroused. Many people crave physical contact, but this is not expected by the Necrophile. The perception of utter and full isolation renders him aroused. His mind obviously has fallen into quite a dark realm.

One of the more despotic personalities manifesting from the other side is the serial murderer. The serial murderer is often a topic of mystery in novels, legal trials, and television reports. The nature of this embodiment of deviant horror reflects a portion of the human mind and can actually be felt only by a serial killer itself. The mass murderer is addicted to homicide, just like the alcoholic covets his next beer or even an opiate abuser craves for the next dose.

The mass murderer thinks of the excitement and enhanced feeling of freedom after his crime is over. Distinctively prolific arsonist or the necrophile, the main purpose of the serial murderer is to quench life. Sexual gratification by tormenting their captives is a favorite subject for them. While a prevalent trend, there are many more troubling drives that trigger their victims to be abused.

Such four representations provide indicators of the degree to which people can strive for control, enjoyment, and/or objective accomplishment encounters. Each of the mentioned criminal profiles includes attackers feeling gratified by their violent and/or heinous acts. The fact is that such descriptions are simply simple portraits of four divisions of the male and female community taking part in violent, harmful, or deviant activities. The degree to which people are going to participate in sexual pleasure, perceived power, or financial advantage is very vast and nuanced.

Since the emergence of scientific progress and society's capacity to understand deviant human conduct, the origin of such confusion was ghosts and demons. Unable to grasp how persons could perform these crimes, the only plausible reason was supernatural entities. Early cultures concocted stories and myths about supernatural creatures instead of being afraid of their neighbors. Werewolves, Witches, and Ghouls stalked their victims through the darkness.

Although mainstream culture regards itself as mature in its capacity to grasp human propensity for violence and horrific activities, it remains difficult to know how to minimize and/or avoid strange and deadly human behavior. Our genus is the sole community of living beings participating in acts that are antithetical to human existence.

10.5 Triad of Dark Psychology

Narcissism- grandiosity, absence of empathy, Egotism.

Machiavellianism– incorporating deception to trick and manipulate individuals, but has no moral sense.

Psychopathy– Usually delightful and pleasant yet described by impulsiveness, irrationality, complete absence of empathy, as well as remorse.

Few of us intend to be the object of abuse, however very frequently, it occurs.

Such strategies are also used in advertisements, online advertising, promotional methods, and also the actions of our boss. When you have children (particularly teenagers), you can more likely witness such strategies when your kids play with actions to acquire what they desire and try autonomy for self. In fact, the people you love and trust often use secretive manipulation as well as dark persuasion. Below are a few of the strategies that ordinary, everyday individuals use most often.

Love Flooding- appreciation, compliments, or buttering others

Lying- falsehoods, Exaggeration, half-truths, fabricated statements

Love Denial- hold back devotion and attention

Withdrawal- silent treatment or ignoring the individual

Restriction of choice- Giving specific choices that divert attention from the option you don't really want anybody to choose.

Reverse Psychology- Speak one thing to the individual or do something with the aim of motivating the others to do the contrary that is truly what you desire.

Semantic manipulation- Use terms that are meant to have a shared or reciprocal sense, but then the manipulator informs you that he or she has a distinct interpretation of the interaction and comprehension. Words are important and powerful.

The object is not to say that how to stop the manipulation and abuse. Rather, that's to show us just how simple it is to use such strategies to achieve what we like. Evaluate the strategies in all aspects of life, such as leadership, intimate partnerships, family, friendship and work, Although those individuals who use dark strategies realize just what they want and are able to exploit you to achieve what they desire, some are utilizing sinister and immoral techniques without being completely conscious of it. Some of these individuals learned techniques from their families during their youth. Others acquired the techniques by sheer coincidence in their adolescent years or teen years. They unintentionally utilized a manipulative tactic, and it worked. We did get what we needed. And they start employing strategies to enable them to achieve whatever they want. Individuals are coached in some instances to use those tactics. Usually, advertising or marketing systems are educational schemes that teach grim, deceptive psychological & persuasive techniques. Some of these services employ dark strategies to build a reputation or market a commodity purely for the sake of supporting themselves as well as their business, not really the consumer. Some of these coaching programs persuade individuals that the usage of these strategies is good and is in the buyer's interest. Since, obviously, as they buy goods or services, their lifestyles must be much easier.

Who is utilizing Dark Psychology as well as the techniques of manipulation? Here are a number of individuals who appear to make the best of such strategies.

Narcissists – Extremely narcissistic individuals (fulfilling clinical verification) with an exaggerated idea of self-pridefulness. They depend on others to justify their verdict that they are superior. They've fantasies of being adored and worshiped. To preserve that, they use techniques of unethical persuasion, manipulation, and dark psychology.

Sociopaths – Those who are genuinely sociopaths (fulfilling clinical verification), are often friendly, articulate, and impulsive. We use sinister strategies to set up a shallow connection and instead take full advantage of others because of a loss of emotional intensity and the desire to show guilt.

Attorneys – Many attorneys dwell on succeeding their lawsuit so eagerly that they turn to use dark persuasion techniques to achieve the verdict they want.

Rulers – Many elected officials adopt dark psychological and sinister strategies of persuasion to persuade people to gain votes.

Sales personnel – Some salespeople are too concentrated about making a deal that they employ dark approaches to inspire and convince someone to purchase their product.

Members– Many leaders utilize dark strategies for the subordinates to gain obedience, better efficiency, or greater effort.

Public Speakers– many presenters choose dark strategies to enhance the audience's emotional state by realizing it tends to lead to more products being sold at the side of the stage.

Selfish individuals– Whoever has a self-goal over anyone would be it. First, they might use tactics to satisfy their own demands, even at the cost of someone else. They don't bother win-losing results.

To discern between those dark strategies of persuasion and motivation & those ethical, it is necessary to determine the purpose. We ought to question whether the strategies we are utilizing aim to benefit the other individual. It's all right for the purpose to be benefiting you too, but when it's all for your gain, you will quickly slip into grim, dishonest activities.

The goal would be to create a mutually advantageous result. Yet you have to be frank about yourself & the assumption that the other party actually does earnings. An indication of that is a seller who assumes that everybody will profit from his goods, and due to the purchase, life would be a lot easier for the consumer. A seller with this attitude will quickly slip for utilizing dark strategies to get the individual to purchase and using a mindset of "end justify the mean." It opens up the customer to any & all strategies to really get the deal.

We should ask the questions to ourselves, with the motivation & persuasion tactics, to determine our intention:

1. What's my purpose for that interaction? How and who gets the benefit?

2. Do I feel comfortable about the way I conduct the conversation?

3. Am I completely transparent and frank?

4. Can the outcome of the interaction contribute to the other person's long-term advantage?

5. Will the strategies I use to contribute towards a more positive partnership with other individuals?

Will you want your management, partnerships, family, job, and other aspects of life to be genuinely successful? Then evaluate yourself to decide your present drive and persuasion strategies. Doing everything right gives prestige and power in the long run. Doing something incorrect (going dark) result in bad character, ruined relationships & long-term defeat as others can inevitably see beyond the darkness & know the purpose.

How can you manipulate the minds of people using dark psychology?

This is both a study of the human experience and a construct of human consciousness as it corresponds to the mental nature of individuals to prey on someone else inspired by psychopathological, psychotic, or depraved unlawful drives which lack objective and particular assertions of science theory, evolutionary biology, and instinctual drives.

10.6 Concept Analysis

We should understand, dark psychology is the power to manipulate the thoughts of others. We also have this ability, and consciously and unconsciously make use of it too. This is a mental game where we compete with the emotions, desires, beliefs, etc. of certain individuals in order to fulfill oneself by attaining desirable goals. We may assume, for instance, that a seller is really excited about marketing his goods to the buyer & uses dark manipulation to exploit the clients. He is deliberately doing so.

At the other side, the selfish person plays the trick with one's subconscious and unknowingly satisfy needs of them. Dark psychology, which occurs unconsciously, can be quite dangerous as it can deeply affect the feelings of others. It's not healthy to deliberately apply to someone, too.

10.7 Darkness Manipulation

It is an unprecedented force exploiting shadow or darkness. That is the reverse of the Light Manipulation.

Its superpower's users can build, form, and control the shadow or darkness for different levels of impact, sizes, intensities, and shapes. Based on the degree of energy, one can easily use this tremendous force to shroud an entire region, nation, or even the planet in everlasting darkness throughout the whole time.

This superpower has some legendary applications such as:

- D. Teach

- Rouge Cheney

- Marshall

- Shunsui Kyoraku & Ichibei Hyosube

- BlackStar

Therefore, this capacity is as productive as one wishes and relies on the consumer for its control.

10.8 Dark Humor and Psychology

Dark humor has become a recent concept in modern psychology. It is a high intellect predictor. There are several examples of black humor such as taboo jokes, as per a new study, "People who enjoy taboo jokes display higher intellect rates."

The understanding of black comedy may be the predictor of intellect rates; the love of the so-called "gallows humor" is related to elevated rates of verbal or nonverbal intelligence as well.

Humor makes a temporary and comparatively healthy release, in the form of laughter, of generally repressed sexual & harmful impulses. Too much work and experimenting are going on with regarding black humor and that dark humor. There is a handful in this universe that has that sort of humor. This provides for a strong degree of intellect.

10.9 Tactics of Dark Psychology

We knowingly see dark psychological strategies in our daily lives. The manipulators secretly strike us, and we couldn't even know it. Manipulators use techniques as a matter of fact, intentionally. Some secret manipulators consciously do and say stuff for influence and leverage to get whatever they want.

The methods of manipulation include implicit violence, criticism, competitive harassment, and indirect kinds of emotional abuse. These are the tools that are commonly used:

1. Making you feel your embarrassment and remorse

2. Whining towards you

3. Equating you against someone

4. To lie and refute

5. Avoiding you

6. Playing around with your subconscious

7. Emotional blackmail

8. Expressing sympathy

9. Apologizing

10. Do yourself favor

These techniques are associated with awareness by manipulators. Such disruptive strategies can be devastating to you, and can also hurt your self-worth. We will figure out how to negotiate with unpleasant and narcissistic individuals for our own self-protection.

10.10 Tricks of Dark Psychology

There are good and bad aspects of every single event in this universe. If we would choose dark psychology to distort the minds of people for something like the benefit of human society, that's going to be great. There are too many dark psychological tricks for someone to exploit. We will use these techniques with simplicity and, of course, knowledge. We ought to note that even when using techniques, not to be the source of some kind of damage to others.

Below are a few tactical strategies and suggestions for controlling the minds of the people.

Let's use them for craft-

1. Keep smiling Before Speaking: It will make everyone feel relaxed with you & eventually open to you.

2. Eye contact: This serves to keep you wise and alert. Others are going to be treating you & your expressions seriously.

3. Being good to others: Say "hi" to your peers and those you meet and develop yourself as the well-behaved citizen to them

4. Choosing phrases or terms wisely: For starters, you would say "you are right" rather than saying, "I agree," and the other individual can feel happier talking to you.

5. Stay quiet: When you don't ask for more details, stay silent, and the other individual will immediately satisfy your hunger. But on the other side, if you decide to escape stilling others, he/she will quit bothering you.

6. Giving others importance: Speaking allows him / her ample space to share his / her view. Heed their remarks closely.

7. Let others be comfortable around you: Say the names of others with love when communicating. Never render a circumstance humiliating. Give them the chance to try to know you.

8. Stop arguing: Don't really attempt to reason because you realize he/she is thinking anything, don't mention anything outright. Let them end and try using constructive terms to get them to realize the truth.

9. Making people happy: When you intend to manipulate someone's mind, you will be capable of making them laugh because laughing makes them weak.

10.Handling offensive individual: Stay silent and only use the very term that would explicitly assault him/her. That way, he/she is going to be commanded.

Secrets of Dark Psychology:

Anyone, including employers, acquaintances, and family members, may be targeted by manipulators that are very near in our everyday lives. We must all be mindful of our negative personalities and avoid getting victimized. You must first be able to defend yourself by information acquisition. So enrich your mind with the help of reading. Therefore you can better support yourself.

What is manipulation by dark psychology?

It's a process through which individuals conduct mind plays with the feelings, desires, ideas, and expectations of others to consciously and unintentionally achieve desirable objectives. Many of us unknowingly practice this art of deception & mind domination. This is an abnormal psychology subject. Every day all kinds of offenses are occurring by incorporating dark psychology knowledge. Each person possesses the ability.

Why would people worry about dark psychology?

Much of the period, dark techniques of psychology are employed unethically by those with or without experience and knowledge. Greater forms of criminals use the strength to satisfy their needs with considerable awareness. They do not really think about emotions or feelings. Cyber-criminals appear at the first position in this regard. The main explanation is that people don't care about it because they don't even have basic information about this psychological concept. Those are the principal cause.

What is the psychological Dark Triad?

This is a psychiatric concept composed of three anti-social behavior characteristics: Psychopath, Machiavellianism, and Narcissism. Despite their wicked attributes, they are known as dark people. It's used in psychology, especially in the areas of clinical psychology, law enforcement, and even business administration.

Chapter 11: NLP

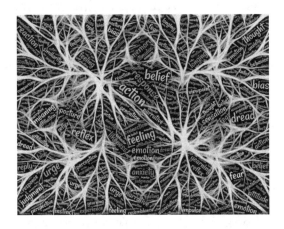

NLP, as the name says, is the program that helps to cope up with the psychological problems. This is a system which helps the expert to read and assess the pattern of human being thoughts and behavior. The experts of NLP can also train the other individuals from this field to get knowledge. I have discussed a few techniques in this chapter to have a clear idea of this system and how it is applied in actual life to get a hold of the system used. There are stages of achievement, as well. By using and reading up on the techniques used can help a person to get help for him or herself.

11.1 What actually is NLP?

NLP is a system of psychological strategies that interact successfully with the unconscious or subconscious minds of the participant. Brain-hax, in contemporary-day language. The final outcome is how you can interact/make the argument/strike a deal/help convince individuals (or oneself) far more successfully. Ironically, dramatically, more strongly on accusation! Neuro: making reference the nerves or neurons, the brain's communication method Linguistic: making reference to dialect Programming: To fix or establish the means stuff operates.

- NLP should be applied for one's own growth, paranoia, and phobias.

- NLP utilizes methods of cognitive, mental, and empathy to make modifying people's feelings and behavior simpler.

- NLP depends on speech recognition, but it must not be mistaken with the processing of natural language and uses the very same term.

- NLP was founded by John Grinder & Richard Bandler, who found it important to recognize the dynamics of effective individuals' thoughts and actions and to introduce these to everyone else.

Despite a lack of scientific data to confirm this, literary works, The Concept of Magic I & II, were written by Grinder and Bandler, and NLP started gaining recognition. The success was attributed in part to its flexibility in grappling with the various complex problems confronted by people.

11.2 What would that be intended for?

Neuro-linguistic programming is a means to alter people's emotions and attitudes and enable them to achieve optimal outcomes.

After it started in the 1970s, the success of neuro-linguistic programming, or NLP, has been broader. The benefits involve managing phobia and anxiety problems and enhancing efficiency in the workspace or personal satisfaction.

How's that working out?

NLP's differing definitions make description challenging. This is focused on the premise that people work from the world's inner "tracks," which they acquire from sensory experiences.

NLP helps to identify and modify latent prejudices or shortcomings of a global map of a person.

NLP aren't hypnotherapies. Alternatively, it operates by deliberately using language to introduce shifts in one's emotions and actions.

A core characteristic of NLP, for instance, is the notion that an individual is skewed against one sensory system, defined as that of a preferred representational system or PRS.

Therapists, by language, may sense the choice. Phrases like "I see your argument" may represent a visual PRS. Or "I perceive your claim" might indicate an audible PRS.

An NLP professional should define the PRS of an individual and build the clinical structure on the condition. The structure may include building partnerships, collecting knowledge, and establishing targets for them.

11.3 NLP Techniques

Neuro-Linguistic Programming became a modeling methodology which provides a toolkit of approaches to address the opportunities and challenges of life. It's a rather realistic science today trying to put outcomes into the modern world.

It begins with a positive mind; we're curious about how stuff works. It also helps one to model effective individuals in a number of scenarios, and such templates are checked and improved constantly.

It, in effect, refers to a range of strategies to replicate and hand onto someone else what is taught.

A model's function is that does that operates in the sense in which we are operating. NLP is a 'pattern, check, optimize, and evaluate method. Even so, it's not a theoretical science, because we rely on what happens, rather than on the idea behind it. We remain up-to-date with science study, though, because it offers rich content for discovery and examination.

Effective NLP preparation would not only demonstrate how to utilize the strategies but will also provide the knowledge and expertise required to adjust them consistently and develop new ones centered on particular clients' different responses.

Why is it so good?

It will help you develop your leadership skills greatly, and can affect them. Practicing these strategies will also improve your endurance and willingness to handle change – like exercising in a gym will develop your muscle power, agility, and stamina.

The strategy will help you dramatically increase the outcomes you produce in the market by having you develop your expertise in leadership, selling, management & relationships. NLP will help you relate to the intent of your private life, resolve obstacles & help you walk the path of your very own superhero.

11.4 What does Neuro-Linguistic Programming imply by these words?

The term neuro-linguistic programming emerged after police detained co-founder Richard Bandler for suspected speeding. He was questioned what his occupation was, and when he looked at the names of both the books he had in his vehicle, he ended up with the answer. Nevertheless, the name provides a good overview of what we are doing.

Neuro means nervous system related. The knowledge that we receive from our perceptions impacts our neuronal work. If we increase the consistency with which we collect knowledge, that is to say, we listen more and become more observant, and we are more responsive to the experience of our own and others. This ensures that our minds have more knowledge that can help them make choices. We are all increasing our capacity to interact (both knowingly and unknowingly) efficiently.

Linguistic implies dialects. If we learn and become more mindful about language – the terms themselves, and also their meaning and the way they are said (velocity, voice sound, rhythm), then we get more knowledge for decision taking and conscious and unconscious contact.

Here programming includes patterns. We are forming patterns, some beneficial ones, other, less helpful ones. NLP shows one how to build and encourage helpful behaviors, and how to popular less productive habits.

Now, you go there: Neural Linguistic Training-using words to train the nervous system towards more efficient patterns. In any case, the performance also requires cultivating the correct behaviors.

11.5 A short overview of Neuro-Linguistic Programming

Neuro-Linguistic Programming first developed by John Grinder & Richard Bandler & more than forty years earlier. They trained and consulted with some of the day's most talented psychologists and therapists: Fritz Perls, Virginia Satir, & Milton Erickson. Nevertheless, compared to other scholars at the moment, they adopted a distinct stance even though they concentrated instead of just theorizing on getting about tangible progress.

Bandler and Grinder needed to learn the best artists using strategic techniques-what they did & also how they managed it. They developed ways to model these techniques so that others could reproduce their success. It was the original NLP pattern.

They then reviewed the concept for their customers and perfected it. When diverse people learned of its advantages, it circulated across a broad range of endeavors of humans, like education, fashion, entertainment, and industry.

NLP has seen a variety of powerful supporters in its existence, and a variety of strong opponents. The critics in the NLP's biggest error for an analytical rather than a modeling profession and the arguments made by certain trainers are a bit too naive and too passionate.

And it's recommended that you perform things with your own initiative before engaging in NLP, finding out whether things are appropriate for you, as well as testing out every mentor or therapist you may be utilizing.

What qualities are required for more exploration and learning?

You don't require any additional credentials. It is discovered, however, that a pinch of imagination, determination, bravery, dedication, and honesty lets individuals produce genuinely good results. You will need to devote the time & mental resources to execute and check what is really being accomplished, as a customer.

11.6 NLP Primary Advantages

Exercising NLP, as well as the NLP Techniques, provides numerous implications that we can discuss in more depth in the papers below. An overview of the major advantages that should be greater than sufficient to have you enthused about the possibility of studying more will suffice for now.

NLP instructs you to:

To connect more. NLP teaches you how to interact in a dialect that aligns with others. That, in effect, helps you to build stronger partnerships and the outcomes you want to achieve! Even NLP lets you grasp what people actually feel by speaking with you. It helps you to become more successful in partnerships, and company-it will also make you learn more about the opposite gender.

Growing motivation. NLP does have a range of methods and strategies that help you become more inspired. With your memories and emotions, you play around for a little bit, which with exercise, enables you to select your mental state more effectively. If in the past you have had difficulty keeping focused, interpret on, because there are some truly straightforward ways to defeat the system here a little bit.

Think favorably. But not in a shallow "all would be perfect if I think about optimistic" fashion – but by creating a better, stronger, more permanent shift within the value structures. It is a Huge NLP Truth-even once you alter your views, the outcomes will alter.

This is an important target on the personal growth path – for as long as you finally begin to realize the NLP Truth that life is an enjoyable set of obstacles and challenges, instead of a never-ending stream of issues and difficulties, items begin to settle into balance and existence becomes Fun.

Adjust behavior. That's NLP's part P. There are a few pretty interesting strategies to incorporate different forms of thought and acting through your mind – so if you're carrying out any of the above techniques, you'll get some really soothing effects. You will become more optimistic, procrastinate less, turn yourself into a convincing motivational narrator, and consider yourself as somebody who merits loads of more cash – in reality because you're just really constrained by your imagination for a lot of the material on this web.

That's a simple overview of NLP/NLP Hidden benefits for you. Another NLP trick – you will create some really incredible improvements in your life even faster than simply utilizing willpower. It is positive news, as improvements achieved purely by determination continue to collapse.

11.7 Five best NLP Tools Transforming the Life

1. Dissociation

Have you really lived in a position when you were feeling bad? Perhaps you've encountered something which would get you off each time you feel it. Or maybe you're getting nervous in some work environments where you possess to talk out in public. Maybe when you desire to reach that "special person" you've will have your eye on, you become shy. Although such emotions of sorrow, shyness or nervousness tend to be inevitable or unavoidable, NLP dissociation strategies may be of tremendous benefit.

1. Classify the emotions (e.g., fear, rage, irritation, a situation dislike) you want to get rid of.

2. Assume you could even glide from your body as well as reflect back on yourself, facing the whole situation from the perspective of an observer.

3. Notice the sensation is changing dramatically.

4. Assume you will fly from your body gazing at yourself for an additional lift, so fly out of your form again, and you smile at yourself and feel for yourself. The dual disconnection should deprive almost any slight situation of the negative feeling.

2. Re-framing content

Attempt this method if you feel down or helpless in a scenario. Re-framing can take every unpleasant scenario to inspire you by having you constructive regarding the sense of the event.

Let's presume you end your love, for starters. At the top, that can sound horrible, so let's re-frame it. What seems to be the advantages of becoming single? You're now accessible to certain future partnerships, for starters. You have the right to do anything you want, anytime you want to. And from this relationship, you have gained important lessons that will enable you to have much better future relationships.

All these are instances of having a situation re-framed. You offer yourself a new understanding of this by re-framing that context of the breakup.

It's normal to worry or dwell on anxiety in planned circumstances, but that just contributes to even more issues. In comparison, turning your attention to the way you have just mentioned helps clear your mind and make rational, even-handed choices.

3. Anchoring Yourself

Centering originates from the Russian psychologist Ivan Pavlov that performed with dogs by constantly circling a bell as the dogs feed. After frequent bell rings, he found that by ringing a bell at any time, he can get the pets to drool, even if there's no meat available.

It produced a neural connection between both the bell as well as salivating actions called a programmed response.

You should use all kinds of "anchors" stimulus-response yourself!

Anchoring yourself lets you connect your desired optimistic emotional reaction to a particular expression or feeling. When selecting a happy emotion or image, then consciously attaching it to a specific action, you will activate this anchor anytime you feel weak, then your emotions will shift automatically.

1. Recognize what you expect to experience (for starters, confidence, joy, peacefulness, etc.)

2. Decide where you like this anchor to be on your body, like grabbing the earlobe, rubbing your thumb, or gripping a fingertip. This body interaction would cause the good feeling to be stimulated at will. Wherever you pick, it doesn't matter

as much as it's a special experience you're not touching for anything specific.

3. Think of a moment in the background where you have known the condition (e.g., confidence). Go back to the period mentally and float through your body, gaze into your eyes & relive the moment. Adapt your physical language to suit state and memory. Look at what you've done, know what you've heard & feel when you recall your memory. You are going to start experiencing the condition. That is equivalent to reading a buddy an amusing tale from memory, so when you "join" the narrative, you start smiling again, as you are "associating" with the tale so "reliving" it.

4. As you return to memory, pull/ touch / shove the area you've chosen on the body. When you reenact the memory, you'll see the sensation swell. The instant the relational condition rises, remove the pressure, and continue wearing off.

5. This will establish stimulus-response neurology that will activate the condition if you render the contact again. Only contact yourself again in the same manner to experience the condition (e.g., esteem).

6. Think of another experience where you feel the condition, look through and revisit it with your eyes, and hold the condition on the same place as before, to make the reaction even better. The anchor gets more effective each time you bring another recollection and will activate a greater reaction.

7. Using this strategy, anytime you want, your attitude modified.

4. Having Anyone like You (Rapport)

This is a simple collection of NLP strategies, but they do have the ability to help almost everyone get on well with you. There are other avenues to establish connections with other individuals. NLP comes as any of the fastest and most powerful forms. Such a method requires a deliberate mimicking of the physical language, voice tone, and vocabulary of another individual.

We prefer others who live who they are. Through unconsciously mirroring other individuals, the brain sets off "mirror nerves," receptors of gratification within the brain that make people feel like someone mirroring them.

The method is easy: Stand up or sit while the other individual sits down. Likewise, raise your cheek. The smile on smiling. Mirror its expression on the face — Mirror the voice, etc.

Subtlety is the secret to establishing an implicit connection. When you're too blatant, the other party may deliberately realize it most definitely ruins the partnership. So hold the mirror-smooth and perfect.

5. Persuasion and Influence

Although most of the NLP's work is devoted to assisting individuals to remove negative feelings, restricting beliefs, unhealthy behaviors, disputes, and much more, a further portion of NLP is devoted to how to impact others ethically and persuade them.

One mentor in the area was a guy called Erickson. He was indeed a psychiatrist that, via hypnotherapy, also researched the subconscious (the real, science material, not the dumb hypnosis of amusement that you view in live performances).

Erickson was really skilled at hypnotherapy, and he devised a way of speaking to other people's subconscious minds without hypnosis. During daily interactions, he might actually hypnotize individuals every moment, wherever. This

Ericksonian hypnosis approach was known as "Conversational Hypnosis."

This is a very effective method that can be used not only to manipulate and motivate people but also to support people to resolve doubts, restrict expectations, disagreement, and so on without conscious knowledge. This is particularly useful when you get through to audiences who would normally be unaware because they teach (think young kids who don't want to hear).

11.8 What Works With Neuro-Linguistic Programming?

Core aspects in neuro-linguistic learning include planning, intervention, and efficient communication. The idea is that if an entity can comprehend how another individual executes a function, then the machine can be replicated and transmitted to others so that they, too, can execute the job.

Neuro-linguistic programming advocates suggest that everybody would have a personal map of the truth. To build a comprehensive summary of one case, those that conduct NLP examine their own from other viewpoints. The NLP patient receives insight from an awareness of a variety of viewpoints.

Advocates in this line in thinking claim that the perceptions are essential to the perception of the knowledge accessible, and also that the mind and body control one another. Neuro-linguistic programming seems to be a methodology that is experiential. Therefore, in order to benefit from the practice, if an individual wishes to comprehend an action, they must conduct the same action.

NLP professionals claim thinking, collaboration, and transformation are inherent hierarchies. The 6 conceptual improvements are:

• **Intent & spirituality:** these can include something greater than one's own, such as faith, philosophy, or any framework. That is the most elevated degree of transition.

• **Identification:** Identification is the individual you claim to be, which involves the responsibilities as well as the positions you perform in life.

• **Convictions and values:** They are the set of moral convictions as well as the questions that matter for you.

• **Talents and competencies:** What are the talents & what you should achieve?

• **Habits:** The basic acts you do are habits.

• **Environment:** The background or atmosphere of the context, or the other individuals around you. This really is the least exchange rate.

Increasing the conceptual level has the function of organizing and coordinating the details beneath. As a consequence, having a lower-level adjustment will trigger higher-level adjustments. Due to the NLP hypothesis, having a difference in such a higher stage would often result in improvements in the lowest stages.

11.9 Neuro-Linguistic Programming In Treatment

The expression, "The graph is not really the territory," will illustrate a central principle of the NLP, as it illustrates the contradictions between perception and fact. This sets out that, instead of from a position of objectivity, each individual works within his own viewpoint. NLP supporters claim that the understanding of the universe for everyone is warped, skewed, and special. Consequently, a practitioner who performs NLP will consider how an individual interprets their "path" in therapy and the impact that interpretation might have on the thoughts and actions of the client.

The world map of an individual is created from data obtained through the perceptions. These may be visual, auditory, gustatory, olfactory, or kinesthetic information. NLP professionals agree that this knowledge varies in aspects of consistency and value internally and that so every individual handles feedback utilizing a PRS. In order for the NLP counselor to function successfully with a healing client, the therapist may seek to fit the PRS of that patient and use their specific chart. NLP professionals agree that the usage of signs such as eye gestures should be utilized to control representational structures.

NLP therapists consult with clients to consider their habits of thought and behavior, their mental status, and their goals. The trainer will encourage them to identify and improve the abilities that better support them by analyzing a person's diagram and enable them to create new approaches to substitute unproductive ones. Its approach will help people achieve recovery milestones in the context of counseling.

NLP proponents say the method provides fast, enduring effects & improves comprehension of behavioral and cognitive trends. NLP frequently helps to create a meaningful dialog between aware & unconscious brain systems to support people to improve imagination & problem - solving abilities. Many NLP proponents equate the method to CBT and argue that there could be significant results in NLP with less time.

Neuro-linguistic learning has been utilized since its introduction to address a wide variety of problems. Including:

- The issues of communication

- deficit-attention hyperactivity

- Fear, anxiety, phobia

- Getting post-traumatic stress

- Schizophrenia

- Depression

- Personality close to the edge

- Addiction

- obsessions & compulsions

11.10 How NLP function in actual life?

Many of us concentrate on verbs through talks. What would this individual mean or in exchange, what do I say? Words have long been recognized as the least important element of speech, expressing just 7% of significance (Mehrabian, 1972).

Of instance, when someone assures you, they're happy to help you arrange a social event, but their tone is hollow, and their face expression feels like you've just asked them to an electric current torture evening. It's evident something different is occurring. Their voices stated yes, yet they meant something else about non-verbal contact – that is the other 93%.

What is actually neuro-linguistic programming? The remaining 93% in communication. This is a framework for knowing and utilizing what other kind of contact is really necessary. Learn nonverbal contact, and you are a master in speech.

But something still more valuable here is:

Many people don't know that contact is made up of so much greater than individual experiences. There is a whole social universe within the body and mind. Inner existence-your mood, mentality, and emotions are important modes of interaction.

The most critical contact is not with individuals but among individuals.

Inner dialog is a strong point in Neuro-Linguistic Programming, initially defined as the study of the contextual perception framework. It is a sophisticated way to suggest the NLP takes down what's going on behind the ears so you can do more positive about it. Here's a glimpse of how it actually functions.

Let's presume that you have buddies over for a meal and that you feel extra nervous. It's not obvious why. Everything is well, but you sound on alert. An NLP professional might work out how, in a few moments, you are producing this stressful condition. It's more about how inwardly you interact about yourself.

The NLP Inner Contact Breakdown

Internal communication consists of pictures, noises, and perceptions (a VAK Model). Figuring out what makes you stressed sensations is a question of searching out which pictures and noises go along with the stressed feeling. When you shift your focus inward, searching internally for whatever you are seeing and hear, you may find that you're thinking about dinner stuff:

- When the visitors come, you see the home all messy.

- A voice inside that states, "They would despise your meal."

- Expressions of disdain as they eat.

- In your room, you're sitting there, because nobody turned up.

So on and so forth. The argument is: You were certainly not fully informed of all the means of internal contact. When you're feeling anxious about dinner, you usually visualize how poorly it might go and react to the implicit sound and imagery. The nervous sensations are a representation of all the various sources.

That is the reason neuro-linguistic programming aims not to break individuals emotionally or mentally. We clearly react to internal contact, whether we are conscious of it or not. And if you imagine negative stuff occurring at your family party, you'll be feeling nervous. You do work well.

You will alter that once you are conscious as to how you build an attitude exactly you do not like. Neuro-linguistic programming provides a wide variety of strategies for modifying our attitude until we recognize it.

The programming element of NLP is to change the internal interaction such that you notice stronger.

NLP Research and Recognition Initiative

Founded by professional psychologist Frank Bourke, is a non-profit group established to extend the scientific study through neuro-linguistic programming.

Bourke earned his Ph.D. in clinical psychology and has been practicing using NLP since the early 1970's.

Dr. Bourke also developed and introduced a recovery program for 800 building residents from the World Trade Center since the 9-11 attack. He found he was ready to change PTSD (trauma) symptoms more rapidly and easily using the NLP-derived treatment than for other therapies.

As a part of this encounter, Bourke created the NLP project to develop the field called neuro-linguistic programming & introduce the work to a professional level that is expected to be applied more broadly.

A popular concern for those pursuing Neuro-Linguistic Programming instruction is, "Is there any work to back up NLP?" A clear majority yes is the resolution. NLP clinicians have been witnessing the findings for decades that are only being formalized as clinical science.

11.11 Anticipates Famous NLP Techniques

Their first finding had been that Satir compared her postulates (verbs, adjectives, and adverbs to that of her visitors without becoming conscious of it. Certain clients will mostly use graphical predicates, whilst some might use kinesthetic or auditory predicates, contributing to the premise that one of the sensations (seeing, listening, or feeling) has been more strongly prized and mirrored in words for every individual.

Once Satir paired her terms with the postulates her patients used, consumers enjoyed Satir's interpretation of them. It built a friendship, rendering her actions quite appropriate.

Eyes Access Cues

Next, Bandler and Grinder found eye-accessing signals that are eye gestures that show that you use images, phrases, and noises, or emotions while you perceive, recall, or understand.

For example, as a right-handed individual looks up at the left, mental memories are usually recalled.

Upon researching Milton Erickson, Bandler and Grinder eventually developed the behavioral techniques utilized by clinicians to change the attitudes of the public efficiently.

Here are the four foundations of neuro-linguistic programming (institutions):

Rapport

The NLP is a major gift for establishing partnerships with others. The partnership can be characterized as being easy to communicate with others. Relationship development promotes confidence in others. Relationships may be established easily through knowing expectations of modalities, eye accessing signs, and predicates.

The Sensory Consciousness

Often you find as you step into someone's home that the colors, tastes, & sounds are very distinct from yours. Neuro-linguistic learning helps you to understand that when you consciously give full notice to your perceptions, the environment becomes far better.

Outcome Thinking

Your aim to achieve something is the outcome. The outcome is related to dreaming towards what you desire, rather than being caught in a pessimistic mode of thought. Outcome strategy concepts can assist in making the right choices and decisions.

Behavioral versatility

Behavioral versatility involves being prepared to do it differently because it does not work the manner you are doing something at present. Flexibility is a critical component of NLP practice. Using NLP lets, you discover new insights in your arsenal and create these patterns.

Skill in Neuro-linguistic Programming

The key reasons an individual may try an NLP coaching includes:

- Be strong, motivating communicator

- Expertise in interpreting non-verbal statements

- Increasing your sensory and subconscious perception;

- Command, and monitor the emotions and thoughts

- Raising suspicions & phobias

- Encourage and inspire

- Develop profound corporate and personal partnerships

- Achieve success & accomplishment

- resolve undesirable habits in and around you

- Communicate effectively and receive knowledge from others

11.12 NLP-Training stages

Most organizations are managing, coordinating, and also accrediting training facilities. Every organization adheres to these following NLP training standards and can be located at various NLP training facilities. This doesn't say, though, that one will transfer from the training facility to the training facility, aiming to achieve the next training level. Training centers also get their courses based on the material of the previous lesson.

So, it is better to either pursue to do all your preparation at one center or to consult with the training sites before beginning your journey.

- NLP Practitioner

- NLP Master Practitioner

- NLP Trainer

- NLP Coach (NCC) is the latest NLP certification level

NLP Practitioner

This is the initial NLP-training level. There's usually no NLP skill prerequisite, so anybody may enroll. An NLP professional preparation involves studying the fundamental aspects of NLP, and also the methods of integrating these aspects with ability and sophistication for use. Such a curriculum includes a set of techniques and performance methods, which bring meaning to life.

This, therefore, involves overcoming problems in partnerships, family business, and learning. Knowing how to overcome these problems results in greater personal development. A professional NLP educator training typically includes real-life NLP Training deployment tasks. Such abilities help us conquer worries & phobias while gaining more trust.

Master of the NLP

An NLP Expert teaching works in greater detail on content at the Practitioner stage or incorporates increasingly specific strategies and templates. Modeling & vocabulary are two of the main things discussed. Individuals learn expertise at this stage to alter attitudes and ideas within themselves & in others, which best suits their life, community, and employment processes. Typically the master curriculum addresses advances in communication methods.

This can involve quantum linguistics, the identification and re-skilling of latent interpersonal strategies, and whether individuals behave differently about how they do so, which is our human beliefs. Training can also include our attitude filters – meta systems that are advanced techniques, specialized NLP mediation skills, sub-modalities, & advanced language negotiation as well.

Every training facility provides its own collection of unique courses. Having a master's program is crucial if your company, well-being, and relations are to be fully transformed. Getting this training allows for significant expansion and benefits.

Trainer of NLP

NLP Trainers teach all NLP Practitioners. The feature enables you to explore your special personality as a teacher and host, which makes a big distinction. A person knows how to be assured, which helps them to get fun in front of others and feel at ease.

Such an experience makes you qualified to be a dynamic and powerful presenter. It offers expertise and strategies for effectively manipulating individuals, recognizing, assessing, and managing community dynamics as well as developing skills for becoming a motivational presenter. Upon completion, the individual will pose with complete trust in the front of audiences of any scale.

Coach of NLP

Any NLP instructor is capable not only of NLP but of Life Coaching as well. During their coaching practices, they use the NLP methods to direct the participant through the phases of a coaching session— Pre talk, Knowledge Collection, Development, and Implementation.

An NLP Instructor may have studied coaching & applied to their expertise on other Mastering and Practitioner credentials. Or, a teacher could have completed a full NLP-Integrated course.

A positive NLP Coach will switch during a coaching session across various strategies and templates, utilizing different ones when appropriate.

NLP Structure Forms Training

Learning in neuro-linguistic training was performed initially in live, community environments. This was felt that the NLP had to be learned to be properly appreciated in person. However, training online has been increasingly common over the decades and also with the growth of the internet, and has become recognized as a successful form of teaching.

For a fact, a combination of private and online instruction is accessible at several centers. Virtual preparation provides other advantages, including the opportunity to study the content and use it in everyday life before going on to other topics and strategies.

Like for all neuro-linguistic programming instruction, though, it needs to suit your particular preferences and needs.

The factors you need to remember when deciding the preparation is appropriate for you:

• The standard of the teachable content

• Their emphasis and their ideology

• Accessibility to fund

• Time needed to fulfill the course(s)

• Integrity of the performance facility and its staff

- Endorsements & Accreditation

- Aid within & post-training

Be sure you pose as many queries as you can to determine how the NLP learning facility fits the standards.